POLISH COOKBOOK

Unleash Your Inner Chef with 365 Days of Traditional Recipes | Delight Your Taste Buds with the Rich Heritage of Polish Cuisine

Zea Mccoy

© Copyright 2023 - All rights reserved. The content contained within this book may not be reproduced, duplicated, or transmitted without direct written permission from the author or the publisher. Under no circumstances will any blame or legal responsibility be held against the publisher, or author, for any damages, reparation, or monetary loss due to the information contained within this book. Either directly or indirectly.

Legal Notice:

This book is copyright protected. This book is only for personal use. You cannot amend, distribute, sell, use, quote, or paraphrase any part, or the content within this book, without the consent of the author or publisher.

Disclaimer Notice:

By reading this document, the reader agrees that under no circumstances is the author responsible for any losses, direct or indirect, which are incurred as a result of the use of the information contained within this document, including, but not limited to, - errors, omissions, or inaccuracies. The information contained in this book and its contents is not designed to replace or take the place of any form of medical or professional advice; and is not meant to replace the need for independent medical, financial, legal or other professional advice or services, as may be required. The content and information in this book have been provided for educational and entertainment purposes only

Table of Contents

INTRODUCTION 8

CHAPTER 1. INTRODUCTION TO POLISH CUISINE 9

1.1 Discovering the Rich Heritage 9

1.2 Essential Ingredients and Techniques 10

CHAPTER 2. APPETIZERS AND STARTERS 12

2.1 Pierogi Magic 12

    2.1.1 Classic Potato and Cheese Pierogi 13

    2.1.2 Mushroom and Sauerkraut Pierogi 14

2.2 Soups That Warm the Soul 14

    2.2.1 Borscht: The Jewel of Polish Soups 15

    2.2.2 Barszcz and Its Variations 16

2.3 Herring and Beyond 16

    2.3.1 Pickled Herring Salad 17

    2.3.2 Tatar: Polish Herring Tartare 18

CHAPTER 3. MAIN COURSES 19

3.1 Hearty Meat Dishes 19

    3.1.1 Bigos: The Hunter's Stew 20

    3.1.2 Kotlet Schabowy and More 21

3.2 Traditional Polish Favorites 21

    3.2.1 Gołąbki: Stuffed Cabbage Rolls 22

    3.2.2 Kielbasa and Sauerkraut Rolls 23

3.3 Fish and Seafood Delights 24

    3.3.1 Karp Po Żydowsku: Jewish-Style Carp 25

    3.3.2 Łosoś z Sosem Koperkowym: Salmon with Dill Sauce 25

CHAPTER 4. SIDE DISHES AND ACCOMPANIMENTS 27

5.1 Comforting Potatoes 27

    5.1.1 Placki Ziemniaczane: Potato Pancakes 28

    5.1.2 Pyzy: Potato Dumplings 29

5.2 The Sauerkraut Connection 29

    5.2.1 Kapusniak: Cabbage Soup 30

    5.2.2 Kielbasa z Kapustą: Sausage with Sauerkraut 31

CHAPTER 5. POLISH DESSERTS AND SWEETS ... 32

6.1 Decadent Cakes and Pastries ... 32
6.1.1 Sernik: Polish Cheesecake ... 33
6.1.2 Napoleonka: Polish Custard Slice ... 33

6.2 Sweet Comforts ... 34
6.2.1 Pączki: Polish Doughnuts ... 35
6.2.2 Makowiec: Poppy Seed Roll ... 35

CHAPTER 6. REGIONAL DELICACIES ... 37

7.1 Tastes of Different Regions ... 37
7.1.1 Silesian Streuselkuchen ... 38
7.1.2 Podpłomyki: Polish Pancakes ... 39

CHAPTER 7. PRESERVES, PICKLES, AND CONDIMENTS ... 40

8.1 Homemade Goodies ... 40
8.1.1 Kisiel: Fruit Jelly Drink ... 41
8.1.2 Kompot: Fruit Compote ... 42

CHAPTER 8. HOMEMADE BEVERAGES ... 43

9.1 Raising a Glass to Tradition ... 43
9.1.1 Kawa z Mlekiem: Coffee with Milk ... 44
9.1.2 Kisiel (Fruit Jelly Drink) ... 45

CHAPTER 9. TRADITIONAL CELEBRATIONS AND HOLIDAYS ... 46

10.1 A Taste of Polish Holidays ... 46
10.1.1 Wigilia: Polish Christmas Eve ... 47
10.1.2 Easter Feasts ... 48

CHAPTER 10. TIPS AND TECHNIQUES ... 49

11.1 Mastering Dumpling-Making ... 50
11.1.1 Rolling, Filling, and Shaping Dumplings ... 50
11.1.2 Boiling, Frying, or Baking Dumplings ... 51

CHAPTER 11. KITCHEN STAPLES AND ESSENTIAL RECIPES ... 53

12.1 Crafting Homemade Pierogi Dough ... 53
12.1.1 Preparing Traditional Polish Sauerkraut ... 54
12.1.2 Creating Your Borscht Base ... 55

CHAPTER 12. HEALTHY TWISTS ON POLISH CLASSICS ... 56

13.1 Lighter Versions of Traditional Favorites 56
    13.1.1 Vegan Cabbage Rolls 57
    13.1.2 Gluten-Free Pierogi Options 58

CHAPTER 13. POLISH FUSION AND MODERN CUISINE 59

14.1 Modern Polish Flair 59
    14.1.1 Contemporary Polish Plating 60
    14.1.2 Fusion Pierogi Creations 61

CHAPTER 14. BRINGING IT ALL TOGETHER 62

15.1 Hosting a Polish Feast 62
    15.1.1 Planning Your Polish Menu 63
    15.1.2 Setting the Table with Polish Flair 64

RECIPES 66

CHAPTER 15. APPETIZERS AND STARTERS 67

1. Classic Potato and Cheese Pierogi 67
2. Mushroom and Sauerkraut Pierogi 69
3. Borscht: The Jewel of Polish Soups 71
4. Pickled Herring Salad 72
5. Tatar: Polish Herring Tartare 73
6. Paszteciki: Polish Pastry Pockets 74
7. Barszcz and Its Variations 76
8. Placki Ziemniaczane: Potato Pancakes 77
9. Pyzy: Potato Dumplings 78
10. Kaszanka: Blood Sausage 79

CHAPTER 16. SOUPS THAT WARM THE SOUL 80

11. Żurek: Sour Rye Soup 80
12. Rosół: Polish Chicken Soup 82
13. Kapuśniak: Cabbage Soup 83
14. Karp Po Żydowsku: Jewish-Style Carp 84
15. Łosoś z Sosem Koperkowym: Salmon with Dill Sauce 85
16. Kapusta kiszona z Grzybami: Sauerkraut Soup with Mushrooms 86
17. Chłodnik: Cold Beet Soup 87
18. Krem z Pieczonych Buraków: Cream of Roasted Beet Soup 88
19. Czernina: Duck Blood Soup 89
20. Kwas Chlebowy: Kvass Soup 90

CHAPTER 17. HEARTY MEAT DISHES: 91

21. Bigos: The Hunter's Stew ... 91
22. Kotlet Schabowy: Polish Pork Cutlet ... 93
23. Gołąbki: Stuffed Cabbage Rolls ... 94
24. Kielbasa and Sauerkraut Rolls ... 95
25. Polskie Kopytka: Polish Potato Dumplings ... 96
26. Jellied Pig's Feet ... 97
27. Kiełbasa Myśliwska: Hunter's Sausage ... 98
28. Polish Meatballs (Klopsiki) ... 99
29. Kaczka Pieczona: Roast Duck ... 100
30. Kotlety Mielone: Polish Meat Patties ... 101

CHAPTER 18. TRADITIONAL POLISH FAVORITES: ... 102

31. Kartoflanka: Potato Soup ... 102
32. Szarlotka: Polish Apple Pie ... 103
33. Flaki: Tripe Soup ... 105
34. Placki Ziemniaczane: Potato Pancakes ... 106
35. Pyzy: Potato Dumplings ... 107
36. Krupnik: Polish Barley Soup ... 108
37. Kielbasa z Kapustą: Sausage with Sauerkraut ... 109
38. Kaczka w Sosie Miodowo-Musztardowym: Duck in Honey Mustard Sauce ... 110
39. Barszcz Wigilijny: Christmas Eve Beet Soup ... 111
40. Zrazy: Polish Beef Rolls ... 112

CHAPTER 19. FISH AND SEAFOOD DELIGHTS: ... 113

41. Śledź w Oleju: Herring in Oil ... 113
42. Karp Pieczony: Baked Carp ... 114
43. Kaszanka: Polish Black Pudding ... 115
44. Tuna Melt Pierogi ... 116
45. Krewetki Marynowane: Marinated Shrimp ... 117
46. Sledzie po Kaszubsku: Herring Kaszubski Style ... 118
47. Sledzie w Oleju: Herring in Oil ... 119
48. Kaczka w Sosie Jablkowym: Duck in Apple Sauce ... 120
49. Miruna: Herring Salad ... 122
50. Krewetki Curry: Shrimp Curry ... 123

CHAPTER 20. SIDE DISHES AND ACCOMPANIMENTS: ... 124

51. Kluski Śląskie: Silesian Dumplings ... 124
52. Kasza Gryczana: Buckwheat Groats ... 125
53. Kopytka: Polish Potato Dumplings ... 126
54. Placki z Jabłkami: Apple Pancakes ... 127
55. Cwikla: Polish Beetroot Horseradish Relish ... 128

56. Kwasnica: Polish Sauerkraut 129
57. Racuchy: Polish Yeast Pancakes 130
58. Kiszona Kapusta: Fermented Sauerkraut 131
59. Zapiekanka: Polish Baguette Pizza 132
60. Surówka z Kapusty: Coleslaw 133

CONCLUSION 134

Introduction

Welcome to the tantalizing world of Polish cuisine, a realm where rich history, hearty flavors, and cherished traditions blend harmoniously. In this cookbook, we invite you to embark on a culinary adventure through the culinary tapestry of Poland, unlocking the secrets of beloved Polish dishes that have been passed down through generations.

Polish cuisine is a reflection of the country's vibrant culture, shaped by its geographical location, agricultural resources, and historical influences. From the fertile fields of Mazovia to the rustic highlands of Podhale, Polish cooking showcases a diverse range of ingredients and techniques that are sure to tantalize your taste buds.

The cornerstone of Polish cuisine is its unwavering commitment to quality and freshness. The Poles take pride in sourcing local produce, succulent meats, and wholesome dairy products, creating a harmony of flavors that are simply irresistible. Whether you're indulging in a hearty pierogi, savoring a bowl of comforting żurek, or relishing a succulent piece of kiełbasa, each bite promises to transport you to the picturesque landscapes of Poland.

In this cookbook, we present a treasure trove of mouthwatering recipes that showcase the essence of Polish cuisine. From traditional classics to modern interpretations, we have curated a collection that caters to both the seasoned home cook and the adventurous food enthusiast. Each recipe is accompanied by step-by-step instructions, helpful tips, and personal anecdotes, ensuring that you can recreate the authentic flavors of Poland in your very own kitchen.

Beyond the delectable dishes, Polish cuisine is deeply rooted in tradition and celebration. From festive holiday feasts to joyful family gatherings, the act of sharing a meal holds a special place in Polish culture. Prepare to be enchanted by the stories, customs, and warm hospitality that accompany these recipes, as they breathe life into each page of this cookbook.

Whether you're longing to reconnect with your Polish roots, curious about exploring a new culinary tradition, or simply seeking to expand your culinary repertoire, "Delicious Polish Flavors: A Journey into Traditional Polish Cuisine" is your gateway to a world of taste, tradition, and togetherness. Join us as we embark on this gastronomic odyssey and discover the magic that lies within the heart of Polish cooking.

Chapter 1. Introduction to Polish Cuisine

Polish cuisine is rich in flavors, hearty dishes, and a reflection of its history and geographical influences. This will delve into the diverse aspects of Polish cuisine, including its traditional dishes, key ingredients, and cultural significance.

One of the hallmarks of Polish cuisine is its emphasis on hearty, wholesome meals. Traditional Polish dishes often incorporate ingredients such as meat, potatoes, cabbage, and grains like barley and rye. These ingredients are used to create delicious and filling meals that are enjoyed by both locals and visitors alike.

Pierogi, perhaps one of the most well-known Polish dishes, are small dumplings stuffed with various fillings such as meat, cheese, or potatoes. These tasty morsels can be boiled, steamed, or fried and are commonly served with sour cream or butter. Another popular dish is bigos, a hearty sauerkraut and meat stew that is often referred to as "hunter's stew." It typically includes a combination of ingredients like sauerkraut, cabbage, bacon, and various types of meat, creating a flavorful and satisfying meal.

Polish cuisine also showcases a variety of soups, with żurek and barszcz being among the most notable. Żurek is a sour rye soup typically made with fermented rye flour and served with diced sausage, hard-boiled eggs, and potatoes. On the other hand, barszcz is a beet soup that can be enjoyed hot or cold and is often accompanied by sour cream and fresh dill.

When exploring Polish cuisine, it's impossible to overlook the importance of bread. Poland is well-known for its wide assortment of bread, with popular varieties including rye, sourdough, and wheat. These breads are a staple in Polish meals and are often used for sandwiches, as an accompaniment to soups, or simply enjoyed on their own.

Furthermore, Polish cuisine showcases a range of delicious desserts and pastries. One such treat is the paczki, a deep-fried doughnut typically filled with sweet fillings like jam or custard. Szarlotka, a traditional Polish apple pie, is another notable dessert that is loved for its sweet and tangy flavors.

In addition to its culinary delights, Polish cuisine holds significant cultural value. The emphasis on sharing meals with family and friends creates a sense of togetherness and fosters strong connections. Traditional Polish meals are often prepared with love and care, reflecting the warmth and hospitality of the Polish people.

Polish cuisine offers a delectable tapestry of flavors and dishes that are deeply rooted in its rich cultural heritage. From the iconic pierogi and bigos to the hearty soups and mouth-watering desserts, Polish cuisine is sure to captivate the taste buds of anyone who has the pleasure to indulge in it. So, whether you're a food lover or an avid traveler, exploring Polish cuisine is an experience that should not be missed.

1.1 Discovering the Rich Heritage

Poland, a country located in Central Europe, is known for its rich and vibrant heritage. Exploring the cultural, historical, and artistic aspects of this nation unveils a deep and fascinating legacy.

One of the key aspects of the Polish heritage is its history. Poland has a long and tumultuous past that shaped its culture and identity. From the medieval period and the glory of the Polish-Lithuanian

Commonwealth to the partitions and the struggle for independence, each era has left its mark on the Polish people. Understanding this history is essential in appreciating the essence of the Polish heritage.

The cultural heritage of Poland is diverse and captivating. Polish folk traditions, such as music, dance, and clothing, have deeply rooted origins and have been passed down through generations. Traditional Polish cuisine, known for its hearty and flavorful dishes, showcases the country's culinary heritage. Pierogi, kielbasa, and bigos are just a few examples of the delicious and unique Polish dishes that have become popular worldwide.

Poland also boasts a rich artistic heritage. The country has produced numerous renowned artists, musicians, and writers throughout history. From composers like Frederic Chopin to painters like Jan Matejko, Polish art has made significant contributions to the global artistic landscape. Literature plays a crucial role as well, with celebrated Polish writers such as Adam Mickiewicz, Henryk Sienkiewicz, and Nobel laureate Wisława Szymborska gaining international recognition.

The Polish heritage is also profoundly influenced by its religious traditions. Poland has a predominantly Catholic population, and religious faith plays a significant role in shaping the national identity. Pilgrimages to sacred sites like the Jasna Góra Monastery in Częstochowa and celebrations of religious holidays form an integral part of the Polish cultural fabric.

In recent times, modern Polish culture has evolved while still maintaining a strong connection to its heritage. The country's film industry, for instance, has gained international recognition with directors such as Roman Polanski and Andrzej Wajda making waves in the international film scene. Polish architecture, both historical and contemporary, showcases the country's unique style and craftsmanship.

Discovering the rich Polish heritage is an enchanting journey into a nation's history, culture, art, and traditions. From its fascinating past to its flavorful cuisine and artistic contributions, Poland offers a diverse and vibrant tapestry of stories and experiences. Exploring and appreciating the Polish heritage is not only a way to understand and connect with a nation, but also a gateway to embracing and celebrating the beauty of diversity.

1.2 Essential Ingredients and Techniques

When it comes to Polish cuisine, there are several essential ingredients and techniques that are commonly used and contribute to its unique flavors. We will delve into these key ingredients and techniques that define Polish cooking.

One of the fundamental ingredients in Polish cuisine is potatoes. Potatoes are widely used in various dishes, such as the popular potato pancakes called "placki ziemniaczane" or potato dumplings known as "kopytka." They are versatile and add a hearty element to many traditional Polish meals.

Another significant ingredient is cabbage. Cabbage is frequently used in Polish cuisine, either as sauerkraut or cooked as a side dish. It is a key component in dishes like "bigos," a traditional Polish stew, and "golabki," which are cabbage rolls stuffed with a mixture of meat and rice.

Meat plays a significant role in Polish cuisine, particularly pork, beef, and poultry. Pork is especially favored, and dishes like "pierogi ruskie" (Russian dumplings) often contain a mixture of ground pork and spices. Sausages, such as kielbasa, are also an integral part of Polish cuisine and are prepared using traditional curing and smoking methods.

When it comes to techniques, one cannot ignore the importance of fermentation. Fermented foods are a significant part of Polish cuisine, providing unique flavors and health benefits. Sauerkraut, for instance, is made by fermenting cabbage, and the process adds a tangy and sour element to many traditional dishes.

Additionally, Polish cuisine incorporates a variety of cooking techniques, including frying, baking, and boiling. Frying is frequently used for dishes like "placki ziemniaczane" or "kotlet schabowy" (breaded pork cutlet). Baking is popular for making bread, cakes, and pastries. Lastly, boiling is commonly used for soups and stews, such as "barszcz" (beetroot soup) and "rosol" (chicken broth).

Polish cuisine has a rich culinary heritage with essential ingredients and techniques that contribute to its unique and flavorful dishes. From potatoes and cabbage to pork and fermentation, these elements combine to create a diverse and delicious array of traditional Polish meals.

Chapter 2. Appetizers and Starters

Appetizers and starters play a significant role in Polish cuisine, as they are an essential part of traditional meals. These dishes, also known as przekąski or zakąski, are served before the main course and are meant to tantalize the taste buds and prepare the palate for the meal to come.

One popular Polish appetizer is the traditional Pierogi, which are dumplings stuffed with various fillings such as cheese, meat, mushrooms, or potatoes. These dumplings are boiled or fried and often served with sour cream or melted butter. Another well-loved starter is Pasztecik, a small pastry filled with a mixture of meat, mushrooms, and onion. It is usually deep-fried until crispy and served piping hot.

Pickled herring, known as śledzie, are another classic Polish starter. These are marinated in a tangy brine and often served with onions and a dollop of sour cream. They are commonly enjoyed during holidays and special occasions. Another popular option is Smalec, which is a spread made from rendered pork fat mixed with chopped onion, garlic, and sometimes bacon. It is typically served on fresh bread or with pickles.

A traditional Polish snack that can also serve as an appetizer is Oscypek. This is a smoked, semi-hard cheese made from sheep's milk. It has a distinctive shape and is often served grilled with cranberry sauce. It is a regional specialty from the Tatra Mountains in southern Poland.

Lastly, Polish cuisine offers a variety of soups that can be served as an appetizer. One well-known option is Barszcz, a beetroot soup served hot or cold with sour cream. Another popular choice is Zupa Ogórkowa, a creamy soup made with pickled cucumbers and often garnished with fresh dill.

Polish cuisine offers a wide range of appetizers and starters that are flavorful and diverse. Whether it be the beloved Pierogi, the delightful Pasztecik, the tangy pickled herring, or the unique Oscypek cheese, Polish appetizers are sure to set the stage for a delicious and satisfying dining experience. So next time you have a Polish meal, don't forget to indulge in these delectable starters!

2.1 Pierogi Magic

Pierogi Magic holds immense importance in Polish cuisine. These delightful dumplings, made from unleavened dough and filled with various savory or sweet fillings, are a culinary tradition that has been passed down through generations. The magic lies in the combination of flavorful fillings, the soft texture of the dough, and the way they are prepared and enjoyed.

Pierogi are deeply rooted in Polish culture and history. They are often served during festive occasions such as holidays, weddings, and family gatherings. The preparation of pierogi involves a labor-intensive process, usually done collectively by family members, creating a sense of unity and togetherness. This communal aspect of making pierogi has become a cherished tradition, strengthening family bonds and preserving cultural heritage.

The versatility of pierogi is another reason for their significance in Polish cuisine. They can be filled with a wide range of ingredients, including potatoes, cheese, cabbage, mushrooms, meat, fruit, and even chocolate. This diversity allows for endless variations, making pierogi suitable for any taste or dietary preference. Whether you prefer a hearty and savory filling or a sweet and indulgent treat, there is a pierogi to satisfy every palate.

Pierogi not only tantalize the taste buds but also serve as a symbol of Polish identity. They represent comfort, home-cooked goodness, and the uniqueness of Polish food culture. The art of making pierogi has been passed down through generations, with each family adding their own touch and keeping the tradition alive. Polish communities around the world also embrace pierogi as a way to connect with their roots and celebrate their heritage.

Pierogi Magic plays a significant role in Polish cuisine. Its importance goes far beyond being just a delicious dish. Pierogi symbolize the essence of Polish culture, family gatherings, and tradition. Their versatility and ability to bring people together make them truly magical. So, the next time you savor a pierogi, remember the rich history and the spirit of togetherness that it represents.

2.1.1 Classic Potato and Cheese Pierogi

Classic Potato and Cheese Pierogi are a beloved and iconic dish in Polish cuisine. These dumplings are made by wrapping a dough pocket around a filling of mashed potatoes and cheese, usually farmer's cheese. They are then boiled and served with various toppings like fried onion, sour cream, or bacon bits.

The importance of Classic Potato and Cheese Pierogi in Polish cuisine cannot be overstated. They are considered a national dish and are deeply ingrained in the culinary traditions and cultural identity of Poland.

One reason for their significance is their historical roots. Pierogi have a long and rich history in Poland, dating back to at least the 13th century. They were initially introduced as a way to incorporate nutritious and filling ingredients, such as potatoes and cheese, into the diet. Over the centuries, they became a staple dish for both everyday meals and special occasions.

Another reason for their importance is the role they play in celebrating Polish culture and tradition. Pierogi-making is often a family affair, and the process of making and sharing pierogi recipes has been passed down through generations. It is a cherished tradition that brings families together and strengthens bonds. Pierogi are also commonly served during holidays, such as Christmas Eve and Easter, further cementing their significance in Polish culture.

In addition to their cultural significance, Classic Potato and Cheese Pierogi are also beloved for their delicious taste and versatility. The combination of the creamy mashed potatoes and tangy cheese creates a savory filling that is both comforting and satisfying. The dough pocket provides a soft and chewy texture that complements the filling perfectly.

Pierogi can be enjoyed in various ways, making them a versatile dish. They can be boiled, fried, or even baked to achieve different textures and flavors. The toppings and accompaniments also offer endless possibilities, allowing individuals to personalize their pierogi experience. From simple sour cream and chives to more adventurous options like caramelized onions or bacon, there is something for everyone's tastes.

Classic Potato and Cheese Pierogi hold immense importance in Polish cuisine. They are not only a delicious and versatile dish but also a symbol of Polish culture and tradition. The history, cultural significance, and widespread love for pierogi make them an integral part of Polish culinary identity. Whether enjoyed at a family gathering or in a cozy restaurant, pierogi are a true culinary treasure that showcases the rich flavors and traditions of Poland.

2.1.2 Mushroom and Sauerkraut Pierogi

Mushroom and Sauerkraut Pierogi are a popular dish in Polish cuisine. These dumplings are made by enclosing a filling of mushrooms and sauerkraut in a thin, unleavened dough and then boiling or frying them. The dish has a long history in Poland and is considered a traditional comfort food.

The importance of Mushroom and Sauerkraut Pierogi in Polish cuisine lies in its cultural significance and the way it reflects the country's culinary traditions. The dish is an essential part of Polish holiday celebrations and family gatherings. It is often served during Christmas Eve dinner, known as Wigilia, and is also a staple dish during other festive occasions.

The combination of mushrooms and sauerkraut in the filling of the pierogi creates a unique and delicious flavor profile. Mushrooms have been a prominent ingredient in Polish cuisine for centuries. They are appreciated for their earthy and umami taste. Sauerkraut, on the other hand, adds a tangy and slightly sour element to the filling.

The pierogi dough is made from a simple mixture of flour, water, and sometimes eggs. The dough is rolled out and then filled with the mushroom and sauerkraut mixture before being sealed and cooked. The dumplings can be boiled, pan-fried, or even baked. They are often served with a dollop of sour cream, which complements the flavors of the filling.

Mushroom and Sauerkraut Pierogi are not only important for their taste but also for the memories and traditions associated with them. Many Polish families have their own recipes that have been passed down through generations, making the dish a cherished part of their culinary heritage. The process of making and enjoying pierogi often involves coming together as a family, with multiple generations working side by side in the kitchen.

In addition to their cultural significance, Mushroom and Sauerkraut Pierogi have gained popularity outside of Poland. They are now enjoyed by people around the world, who appreciate the simplicity and comforting flavors of this traditional Polish dish. Pierogi festivals and events are held in various countries, showcasing the diversity of fillings and cooking styles.

Mushroom and Sauerkraut Pierogi are an important and beloved dish in Polish cuisine. Their cultural significance, delicious flavors, and tradition of bringing families together make them a treasure of Polish culinary heritage. Whether enjoyed during holiday festivities or as a comforting meal, Mushroom and Sauerkraut Pierogi continue to be appreciated both in Poland and beyond.

2.2 Soups That Warm the Soul

Soups that warm the soul are an integral part of Polish cuisine. In Poland, soups hold a special place in the culture and are a staple in daily meals. These hearty and comforting dishes not only satisfy hunger but also provide nourishment and warmth, especially during the cold winter months.

One of the most famous Polish soups is the traditional Polish Żurek. Made from fermented rye flour, it has a distinct sour taste that is both unique and delicious. It is often served with a hard-boiled egg, sausage, and potatoes, adding texture and depth to the dish. The Żurek is not just a soup; it is a symbol of Polish traditions and heritage.

Another popular soup in Poland is Barszcz. This beetroot-based soup is well-known for its rich crimson color and tangy flavor. It is usually garnished with sour cream and served with traditional Polish pancakes known as "naleśniki." Barszcz not only warms the body but also uplifts the spirit with its vibrant hues and refreshing taste.

Another noteworthy soup in Polish cuisine is the Rosół. This clear broth soup is often made with chicken or beef, simmered slowly to extract maximum flavor. It is commonly served with homemade noodles or dumplings, adding a satisfying texture to each spoonful. Rosół is not only considered a comfort food but also a remedy for common ailments, as it is believed to have healing properties.

In addition to these iconic soups, Poland offers a wide variety of regional soups. Each region has its own unique soup recipes, highlighting local ingredients and culinary traditions. From the hearty and meaty Bigos Soup of Silesia to the delicate and creamy Krupnik Soup of Mazovia, Polish soups cater to diverse tastes and preferences.

Soups that warm the soul play an important role in Polish culinary culture. They bring families and communities together, serving as a centerpiece of gatherings and celebrations. These soups not only provide nourishment but also carry the legacy of Polish traditions through generations.

Soups that warm the soul have a special place in Polish cuisine. They are more than just a meal – they are a reflection of Polish heritage, traditions, and the importance of family. Whether it's the sour taste of Żurek, the vibrant color of Barszcz, or the comforting broth of Rosół, Polish soups are a true delight that warms both the body and the heart.

2.2.1 Borscht: The Jewel of Polish Soups

Borscht is a traditional Polish soup that holds an important place in Polish cuisine. This vibrant and flavorful soup has been a staple in the country for centuries and is loved by both locals and tourists alike.

One of the key factors that contribute to the importance of borscht in Polish cuisine is its rich history. It is believed that borscht originated in ancient times and has been passed down through generations. This soup has become a symbol of Polish heritage and tradition, representing the country's culinary identity.

The ingredients used in borscht also play a significant role in its importance. The base of the soup is typically made from beetroots, which give it its distinctive deep red color. The addition of other vegetables such as carrots, potatoes, and cabbage adds complexity and depth to the flavor profile. Herbs and spices like dill, garlic, and bay leaves further enhance the taste.

The versatility of borscht is another reason why it is highly regarded in Polish cuisine. It can be served either hot or cold, making it suitable for different seasons and preferences. It can be enjoyed as a standalone meal or as a starter before a main course. Borscht can also be customized by adding sour cream or garnishing it with fresh herbs, allowing for personalization and variation in taste.

Borscht is not only beloved for its taste but also for its health benefits. The use of fresh vegetables packed with essential nutrients makes it a nutritious choice. Beetroots, for example, are known for their antioxidant properties and are believed to have various health benefits, such as improving cardiovascular health and boosting the immune system.

In addition, the cultural significance of borscht cannot be overlooked. It is often associated with family gatherings and celebrations, where it is prepared with love and shared among loved ones. Borscht has become a symbol of unity and togetherness in Polish culture, bringing people together through the joy of food.

Borscht holds immense importance in Polish cuisine. Its deep roots in history, flavorful ingredients, versatility, health benefits, and cultural significance contribute to its status as the jewel of Polish soups. Whether enjoyed in the comfort of one's home or experienced in a traditional Polish restaurant, borscht continues to capture the hearts and palates of people around the world.

2.2.2 Barszcz and Its Variations

Barszcz is a traditional Polish soup that holds great importance in Polish cuisine. This beetroot soup has a vibrant red color and a tangy flavor that is beloved by many. Barszcz is not only a delicious dish but also a symbol of Polish culture and heritage.

One of the main variations of Barszcz is the clear Barszcz, also known as Barszcz Biały. This version omits the beets and instead focuses on the essence of fermented rye flour. It has a subtle sour taste and is often enjoyed during Easter festivities. Clear Barszcz represents purity and renewal, as it is usually served as a cleansing soup before indulging in a festive feast.

Another popular variation is Barszcz Czerwony, which translates to "Red Barszcz." This is made with beets as the main ingredient, giving it its signature red color. Barszcz Czerwony is commonly served with sour cream and accompanied by a side of uszka (small mushroom-filled dumplings) during Christmas Eve dinner, known as Wigilia. It is believed that the vibrant red color of this soup brings good luck and prosperity for the upcoming year.

Barszcz is not only delicious but is also regarded for its health benefits. Beetroots, the primary ingredient in Barszcz Czerwony, are highly nutritious, rich in vitamins, and have antioxidant properties. This soup is low in calories and packed with essential minerals and dietary fiber. It is often recommended for detoxifying the body and improving digestion.

Polish cuisine showcases the importance of Barszcz through various traditions and occasions. It is a soup that has the power to bring people together and create a sense of nostalgia. From family gatherings to festive celebrations, Barszcz holds a special place on every Polish table.

Barszcz and its variations have a significant role in Polish cuisine. This beloved soup not only satisfies taste buds but also represents Polish traditions, culture, and health-consciousness. Its unique flavors and vibrant colors make Barszcz an integral part of Polish culinary heritage.

2.3 Herring and Beyond

Herring plays a significant role in Polish cuisine, going beyond just being a popular ingredient. It holds historical and cultural importance and has become a staple in many traditional recipes. The Polish have been fishing and preserving herring for centuries, and it has played a vital role in their diet.

One of the reasons herring is highly valued in Polish cuisine is its versatility. It can be prepared and served in various ways, allowing for a wide range of delicious dishes. Some popular preparations include pickling, smoking, baking, frying, and marinating. Each method enhances the flavor and texture of the fish, making it an integral part of many Polish recipes.

Polish cuisine is known for its hearty and comforting dishes, and herring fits perfectly into this category. It adds depth and complexity to many traditional Polish recipes, such as herring in sour cream sauce (śledź w śmietanie), herring salad (śledź po japońsku), and herring tartare (śledź tatara). These dishes are enjoyed during special occasions and holidays, bringing people together to celebrate and indulge in their rich flavors.

Beyond its culinary significance, herring holds cultural importance in Poland. It symbolizes prosperity and good luck, particularly during Christmas and New Year's Eve celebrations. It is common to find herring-based dishes on the festive table, representing abundance and the hope for a prosperous year ahead.

Additionally, herring played a crucial role in the diet of the Polish people during times of hardship and scarcity. Especially during World War II and post-war periods, herring became an affordable and readily available source of sustenance. Its accessibility and nutritional value made it an essential part of the Polish diet during these challenging times.

Herring is not only regarded for its taste but also for its health benefits. It is rich in omega-3 fatty acids, which are essential for heart health and overall well-being. Including herring in the Polish diet provides a source of these important nutrients, contributing to a balanced and nutritious meal.

Herring holds a special place in Polish cuisine, representing both culinary and cultural significance. Its versatility, rich flavors, and health benefits make it a cherished ingredient in traditional Polish recipes. Whether enjoyed during festive occasions or as a part of everyday meals, herring continues to be an integral part of Polish culinary heritage.

2.3.1 Pickled Herring Salad

Pickled herring salad holds significant importance in Polish cuisine. This traditional dish has been cherished for generations and continues to be a staple in Polish households. The combination of pickled herring, vegetables, and a tangy dressing creates a unique flavor profile that is adored by locals and visitors alike.

The origins of pickled herring salad can be traced back to the coastal regions of Poland, where herring is abundant. Herring has been a vital part of Polish cuisine for centuries, owing to its high nutritional value and availability in the Baltic Sea. The process of pickling herring involves soaking it in vinegar or brine, which adds a piquant and savory taste to the fish.

The salad is typically made by combining pickled herring with various ingredients such as onions, apples, pickles, and sour cream. The combination of sweet, tangy, and salty flavors creates a harmonious taste that is both refreshing and satisfying. This unique blend of ingredients exemplifies the creativity and versatility of Polish cuisine.

Pickled herring salad is often served as an appetizer or as part of a traditional Polish meal. It is commonly enjoyed during special occasions and holidays such as Christmas and Easter. The salad's vibrant colors and bold flavors make it a visually appealing and appetizing addition to the dining table.

In addition to its delectable taste, pickled herring salad offers several health benefits. Herring is a rich source of omega-3 fatty acids, which are essential for cardiovascular health and brain function. The vegetables and fruits added to the salad provide vitamins, minerals, and dietary fiber, contributing to a well-balanced meal.

The significance of pickled herring salad in Polish cuisine goes beyond its culinary appeal. It reflects the cultural heritage and traditions of the Polish people. The dish symbolizes unity, family gatherings, and the preservation of ancestral recipes. It acts as a link between generations, with grandmothers passing down their treasured recipes to their grandchildren.

Pickled herring salad holds a special place in Polish cuisine. Its unique combination of ingredients, distinctive flavors, and cultural significance make it a beloved dish. Whether enjoyed during festive celebrations or as a regular part of the Polish table, pickled herring salad represents the enduring culinary traditions and rich heritage of Poland.

2.3.2 Tatar: Polish Herring Tartare

Tatar: Polish Herring Tartare is a traditional dish in Polish cuisine that holds great importance in the culinary heritage of Poland. This delightful delicacy showcases the harmonious blend of flavors and textures that Polish cuisine is renowned for.

One of the key components of Tatar: Polish Herring Tartare is the herring itself. Herring has been a staple in Polish cuisine for centuries, as Poland has a long coastline along the Baltic Sea. The herring is known for its rich, oily flesh and distinctive taste. It is minced and mixed with various ingredients to create a flavorful tartare.

The tartare is typically made by combining minced herring with finely chopped onions, pickles, and hard-boiled eggs. These ingredients add both crunch and acidity to the dish, creating a balanced and refreshing flavor profile. Additionally, the tartare is seasoned with salt, pepper, and often a touch of mustard, which further enhances the taste.

Tatar: Polish Herring Tartare is served chilled and is commonly enjoyed as an appetizer or a light lunch. It is often presented in an eye-catching manner, either molded into a shape or elegantly arranged on a plate. Some variations of the dish may include additional ingredients such as capers, fresh herbs, or sour cream, adding further complexity to the taste.

This dish holds a special place in Polish cuisine as it represents the cultural and historical significance of herring in the country. Herring fishing has been a crucial industry in Poland throughout the ages, providing a livelihood for many communities along the coast. Tatar: Polish Herring Tartare serves as a tribute to this heritage and is a celebration of the flavors of the sea.

Furthermore, Tatar: Polish Herring Tartare reflects the Polish culinary philosophy, which emphasizes the use of fresh, seasonal ingredients. The dish showcases the natural flavors of herring and the complementary ingredients, allowing each element to shine. It is a testament to the simplicity and elegance that defines Polish cuisine.

Tatar: Polish Herring Tartare holds a significant place in Polish cuisine due to its historical, cultural, and culinary importance. This dish not only showcases the flavors of the sea but also represents the pride and heritage of the Polish people. Its delightful combination of herring, onions, pickles, and eggs creates a harmonious balance of flavors, making it a beloved and timeless dish in Poland.

Chapter 3. Main Courses

Main Courses hold great importance in Polish Cuisine. Poland has a rich culinary heritage with a wide variety of traditional dishes that are savored by locals and appreciated by visitors from around the world. Main Courses often form the heart of a Polish meal, providing nourishment, flavor, and a sense of tradition.

One of the most popular main courses in Polish Cuisine is Bigos, also known as Hunter's Stew. It is a delicious combination of sauerkraut, different types of meat (like pork, beef, or sausage), mushrooms, and aromatic spices. Bigos is often cooked slowly, allowing the flavors to meld together, resulting in a hearty and satisfying dish.

Pierogi is another main course that is beloved in Poland. These dumplings are made with a variety of fillings such as potatoes and cheese, sauerkraut and mushrooms, or meat. Pierogi can be boiled, fried, or baked, and they are usually served with sour cream or melted butter. They are a staple food in Polish households and are often enjoyed during special occasions and holidays.

Polish Cuisine is also known for its assortment of meat dishes. Kotlet Schabowy, similar to the Austrian Wiener Schnitzel, is a breaded pork cutlet that is pan-fried until golden and crispy. It is often served with mashed potatoes, sautéed cabbage, or pickles. Another popular meat dish is Gołąbki, which is cabbage rolls stuffed with a mixture of ground meat, rice, and spices, and then baked in tomato sauce.

Zurek is a traditional Polish soup that can also be considered a main course due to its hearty nature. It is made with sourdough rye flour and seasoned with smoked sausage, bacon, and marjoram. Zurek is often served in a bread bowl, which adds to the uniqueness of the dish.

In addition to these main courses, Polish Cuisine offers a wide variety of dishes that highlight the use of local and seasonal ingredients. From roasted meats like roasted duck or roasted pork ribs, to potato dishes like placki ziemniaczane (potato pancakes) or pyzy (dumplings), main courses in Polish Cuisine showcase the flavors and traditions of the country.

Main courses in Polish Cuisine are not only about sustenance but also about bringing people together. Meals in Poland are often enjoyed in a communal setting, where family and friends gather to share delicious food and create lasting memories. The importance of main courses in Polish Cuisine lies not just in their taste, but also in the sense of togetherness and cultural heritage they represent.

3.1 Hearty Meat Dishes

Hearty meat dishes are an integral part of Polish cuisine and hold great importance in its culinary tradition. These dishes, known for their rich flavors and comforting nature, play a significant role in Polish culture and are often enjoyed during family gatherings, celebrations, and traditional festivals.

One of the most iconic hearty meat dishes in Polish cuisine is "bigos," a flavorful cabbage stew made with a variety of meats such as pork, beef, and sausages. Bigos is considered a national dish in Poland and is often prepared for special occasions. Its long cooking process allows the flavors to meld together, creating a mouthwatering combination of tender meat, sauerkraut, mushrooms, and spices. The result is a hearty and satisfying dish that exemplifies the essence of Polish cuisine.

Another popular dish is "pierogi," which are traditional Polish dumplings filled with different types of meat. The most common fillings include ground pork, beef, or a blend of both. Pierogi can be boiled, baked, or fried, and are often served with sour cream or fried onions. These delicious dumplings are a true comfort food and are enjoyed by people of all ages in Poland.

Polish sausages, or "kielbasa," are also highly regarded in the Polish culinary repertoire. There are numerous varieties of kielbasa, each with its own unique flavor profile. These sausages are made from a mixture of pork, beef, or veal, and are seasoned with garlic, salt, and pepper. They can be grilled, fried, or smoked, and are commonly served with sauerkraut or mustard. Kielbasa is a staple in Polish cuisine and is often enjoyed during barbecues or as a delicious addition to hearty meat dishes.

Additionally, Polish cuisine features dishes like "schabowy," a breaded pork chop, and "golonka," a pork knuckle stewed with vegetables and spices until tender. These dishes showcase the Polish love for meat and their dedication to creating hearty and flavorful meals.

The importance of hearty meat dishes in Polish cuisine goes beyond satisfying hunger. These dishes are a reflection of Polish culture, tradition, and the country's agricultural heritage. As a predominantly agricultural nation, Poland has a long history of livestock farming, which has shaped its culinary traditions. Hearty meat dishes highlight the abundance of high-quality meat and the resourcefulness of Polish cooks in creating delicious meals.

Moreover, these dishes bring people together. In Poland, preparing and sharing a meal is seen as an expression of love and hospitality. Gathering around a table filled with hearty meat dishes creates a sense of togetherness and fosters a strong sense of community. Whether it's a family dinner or a festive occasion, Polish meat dishes contribute to the overall atmosphere and create treasured memories.

Hearty meat dishes play a vital role in Polish cuisine, representing the rich flavors and cultural heritage of the country. From the iconic bigos to the comforting pierogi and flavorful kielbasa, these dishes are cherished and enjoyed by many. They bring people together, celebrate tradition, and provide nourishment and satisfaction. Polish cuisine would not be complete without its hearty meat dishes.

3.1.1 Bigos: The Hunter's Stew

Bigos, also known as the Hunter's Stew, is a traditional dish that holds great significance in Polish cuisine. This will delve into the importance of Bigos and its cultural and culinary significance in Poland.

Bigos is a hearty and flavorful dish that dates back to medieval times and has been an integral part of Polish cuisine ever since. It is a stew made with various ingredients, including sauerkraut, fresh cabbage, different cuts of meat such as pork, beef, and sausage, as well as an assortment of spices such as bay leaves, juniper berries, and pepper. The combination of these ingredients gives Bigos its distinct taste and aroma.

One of the reasons why Bigos is so important in Polish cuisine is its connection to tradition and heritage. In Poland, Bigos is often served during special occasions, such as weddings, holidays, and family gatherings. It brings people together and creates a sense of unity and nostalgia. The preparation of Bigos is often a family affair, with each household having its own unique recipe and techniques passed down through generations.

Beyond its cultural significance, Bigos is also known for its nutritional value. The combination of sauerkraut and fresh cabbage provides a rich source of vitamins and dietary fiber. The different cuts of meat add protein and essential minerals, making Bigos a satisfying and nourishing dish. Additionally, the slow cooking process allows the flavors to meld together and develop a depth that is truly satisfying to the palate.

Bigos also represents the resourcefulness and adaptability of Polish cuisine. Originally, Bigos was a way to preserve leftover meats and vegetables during long winters. The combination of sauerkraut and other ingredients created a dish that could be enjoyed for an extended period of time. Today, Bigos is still a popular choice during the winter months, but it is also enjoyed year-round due to its delicious taste and cultural significance.

Bigos holds great importance in Polish cuisine. Its rich history, cultural significance, and nutritional value make it a cherished dish in Poland. Whether enjoyed during special occasions or as a comforting meal on a cold winter's day, Bigos represents the heart and soul of Polish culinary tradition. It is a dish that brings people together, celebrates heritage, and showcases the adaptability of Polish cuisine.

3.1.2 Kotlet Schabowy and More

Kotlet Schabowy, also known as Polish pork cutlet, and More are two important dishes in Polish cuisine. They hold great significance and are widely loved by the Polish people.

Kotlet Schabowy is a traditional Polish dish made of breaded pork cutlets. The cutlets are first tenderized and then coated with breadcrumbs before being fried until golden brown. The result is a crispy exterior with a juicy and flavorful interior. It is often served with mashed potatoes, sauerkraut, and a side of salad. This dish is considered a classic comfort food in Polish households and is commonly served for lunch or dinner.

The importance of Kotlet Schabowy in Polish cuisine lies in its cultural significance. It showcases the Polish tradition of enjoying hearty and delicious meals. It is a favorite among both young and old generations and is often associated with family gatherings and celebrations. Many Poles have fond childhood memories of enjoying Kotlet Schabowy prepared by their grandparents or parents.

More, on the other hand, is a traditional Polish dish made of a mixture of ground meat (usually pork or veal), onions, bread, eggs, and spices. It is shaped into small meatballs or patties and then simmered in a flavorful broth. More is often served with boiled potatoes and a side of pickles or sauerkraut.

More holds a special place in Polish cuisine as it represents the use of simple and affordable ingredients to create a delicious and satisfying meal. It is often enjoyed as a main course but can also be served as an appetizer or a side dish. More is considered a comfort food and is commonly prepared for family meals or holiday celebrations.

Both Kotlet Schabowy and More reflect the rich culinary traditions of Poland and are loved by locals and visitors alike. They showcase the use of traditional ingredients and cooking techniques that have been passed down through generations. These dishes not only offer a delightful gastronomic experience but also serve as cultural symbols, representing the pride and love for Polish cuisine.

3.2 Traditional Polish Favorites

Traditional Polish favorites play a significant role in the Polish cuisine. These classic dishes are not only delicious but also represent the rich cultural heritage of Poland.

One of the most famous traditional Polish favorites is pierogi. These dumplings are made with a simple dough and filled with a variety of ingredients such as potatoes, cheese, sauerkraut, or meat. Pierogi are typically boiled and then fried with butter and onions. They are a staple in Polish households and are often enjoyed as a main course or a side dish.

Another beloved Polish dish is the bigos, also known as hunter's stew. This hearty and flavorful dish is made with sauerkraut, fresh cabbage, various types of meat (such as pork, beef, and sausages), and an assortment of spices. Bigos is cooked slowly over a long period to allow the flavors to meld together. It is usually served with rye bread and is a popular choice during social gatherings and holidays.

Polish cuisine is also known for its wide selection of soups, with żurek being one of the most famous. This sour rye soup is made with fermented rye flour, smoked bacon, potatoes, and sausage. It has a tangy, slightly sour taste that is unique and delicious. Żurek is often served with a hard-boiled egg or a dollop of sour cream to enhance the flavor.

Besides these, there are numerous other traditional Polish favorites that are cherished by locals and visitors alike. Krokiety are crispy rolled pancakes filled with various savory fillings, such as mushrooms, meat, or cheese. Polish sausages, or kiełbasa, come in different varieties and are a staple ingredient in many dishes. Polish pancakes, known as naleśniki, are thin crepes that can be enjoyed with sweet or savory fillings. Lastly, Polish apple pie, called szarlotka, is a beloved dessert made with a buttery crust and a generous amount of cinnamon-spiced apples.

The importance of these traditional Polish favorites goes beyond just their taste. They represent the cultural identity of Poland and are a source of pride for the Polish people. These dishes have been passed down through generations and are deeply rooted in Polish tradition and history.

Traditional Polish favorites are a significant part of Polish cuisine. They not only offer a delightful gastronomic experience but also showcase the rich heritage and cultural diversity of Poland. Whether it is the comforting pierogi, the hearty bigos, or the flavorful żurek, these dishes are cherished by locals and continue to be celebrated as an important part of Polish culinary tradition.

3.2.1 Gołąbki: Stuffed Cabbage Rolls

Gołąbki, also known as stuffed cabbage rolls, hold great significance in Polish cuisine. These traditional delicacies are made by filling steamed cabbage leaves with a savory mixture of ground meat, rice, and fragrant spices. The rolls are then simmered in a flavorful tomato sauce until tender and irresistibly delicious.

The importance of gołąbki in Polish cuisine is rooted in their rich cultural heritage. They have been cherished for generations, passed down from one family to another, and enjoyed during festive occasions and family gatherings. Gołąbki represent a connection to Polish traditions and are a symbol of Polish culinary excellence.

One of the reasons why gołąbki are highly regarded in Polish cuisine is their versatility. They can be made with various fillings and different types of cabbage, such as green or white cabbage. This flexibility allows for creativity and experimentation in the kitchen, resulting in countless delicious variations.

Gołąbki are not just a beloved dish; they also reflect the resourceful nature of Polish cooking. Historically, these cabbage rolls were prepared in large quantities during harvest time to make the most of seasonal vegetables. This practical approach to cooking demonstrates the Polish people's ingenuity in maximizing ingredients and minimizing waste.

Furthermore, gołąbki embody the flavors and aromas that are distinctly Polish. The combination of savory meat, tender cabbage, and aromatic spices like bay leaves and allspice creates a comforting and satisfying culinary experience. The layers of flavors and textures harmoniously come together, making each bite a delightful journey for the taste buds.

In addition to their cultural and culinary significance, gołąbki hold a special place in the hearts of many Polish individuals. They evoke memories of family gatherings, holiday celebrations, and cherished moments spent around the dining table. These stuffed cabbage rolls represent the warmth and love found in Polish homes, creating a sense of nostalgia and fondness.

Gołąbki: stuffed cabbage rolls, are an integral part of Polish cuisine. They not only showcase the culinary expertise of Polish cooks but also embody the country's cultural heritage. These versatile, delicious, and nostalgic dishes bring people together, creating lasting memories and a deep appreciation for the importance of food in Polish culture.

3.2.2 Kielbasa and Sauerkraut Rolls

Within the rich and diverse culinary traditions of Poland, Kielbasa and Sauerkraut Rolls hold a special place of importance. These iconic and flavorful rolls are a testament to the centuries-old culinary heritage of Poland and its deep-rooted appreciation for hearty and delicious dishes.

Kielbasa, a type of traditional Polish sausage, forms the heart and soul of Kielbasa and Sauerkraut Rolls. Made from a blend of high-quality meats, typically pork, beef, or a combination of the two, and flavored with a variety of herbs and spices, Kielbasa encapsulates the essence of Polish cuisine. Its robust and savory flavors are often a result of the unique smoking and curing techniques employed by Polish butchers. The distinctive smokiness of Kielbasa contributes greatly to the overall taste profile of the rolls.

Partnered with the flavorful Kielbasa is another quintessential ingredient in Polish cuisine—the Sauerkraut. Sauerkraut, fermented cabbage, brings a tangy and slightly sour element to the dish. The fermentation process not only enhances the flavor but also offers numerous health benefits. With its high content of vitamins, minerals, and probiotics, sauerkraut promotes a healthy digestive system and boosts the immune system. The combination of Kielbasa and Sauerkraut results in an unforgettable flavor harmony that has delighted Polish palates for generations.

The process of making Kielbasa and Sauerkraut Rolls is a labor of love that requires culinary skill and expertise. The preparation begins with the selection of the finest ingredients, ensuring the utmost quality and taste. The Kielbasa is typically sliced and briefly sautéed to enhance its flavors and bring out its natural juices. The Sauerkraut, on the other hand, is rinsed and cooked to reduce the sourness while retaining its signature tang.

Once the ingredients are prepared, the rolls are meticulously assembled. A generous portion of cooked Sauerkraut is placed on a slice of Kielbasa, which is then rolled tightly in a soft and fluffy dough. The rolls are then baked to perfection, resulting in a golden-brown exterior that envelops the succulent Kielbasa and tender Sauerkraut filling. The warmth and aroma that emanate from the oven during the baking process have the power to evoke fond memories and create a cozy atmosphere.

The significance of Kielbasa and Sauerkraut Rolls in Polish cuisine extends beyond its flavor profile. It serves as a cultural symbol, representing the resilience and creativity of the Polish people. Just like the rolls themselves, the Polish culture is a blend of various influences and traditions, blending harmoniously to create something uniquely beautiful.

These rolls are not merely a culinary delight but also possess a social dimension. In Poland, Kielbasa and Sauerkraut Rolls are often enjoyed during family gatherings, holidays, and festive celebrations. They bring people together, fostering a sense of unity, and creating cherished memories shared around the dining table. The act of preparing, serving, and savoring these rolls has become a cherished tradition, passed down from one generation to the next.

Kielbasa and Sauerkraut Rolls are an integral part of Polish cuisine, both in terms of taste and cultural significance. The combination of the smoky and savory Kielbasa with the tangy and vibrant Sauerkraut creates a harmonious flavor profile that represents the essence of Polish culinary traditions. Beyond the culinary realm, these rolls foster a sense of community and togetherness, transcending mere ingredients to become a symbol of Polish heritage and tradition.

3.3 Fish and Seafood Delights

Fish and Seafood Delights play a significant role in Polish Cuisine. Poland, being a country surrounded by several bodies of water, has abundant access to fish and seafood, making it an essential part of their traditional dishes.

One of the most popular fish dishes in Poland is Smoked Salmon (Wędzony Łosoś). It is often served as an appetizer or incorporated into sandwiches and salads. Smoked salmon is marinated and then smoked over wood chips, resulting in a delicate and smoky flavor that adds depth to any dish.

Another iconic Polish seafood dish is Fisherman's Soup (Zupa Rybna). This hearty soup is made by simmering various types of freshwater fish with vegetables, herbs, and spices. It showcases the rich flavors of different fish species, creating a savory and satisfying dish.

Polish Cuisine also features numerous seafood delights, including Baltic Herring (Śledź Bałtycki) and Carp (Karp). Baltic Herring, a popular fish found in the Baltic Sea, is often marinated in a mixture of vinegar, onions, and spices, creating a tangy and refreshing appetizer or side dish. Carp, another traditional Polish fish, is famously served during Christmas Eve dinners. It is prepared in various ways, such as breaded and fried or baked with vegetables, and holds great cultural significance.

In addition to these popular dishes, Polish Cuisine incorporates fish and seafood into diverse recipes such as Pierogies (dumplings) filled with fish or seafood, Fish Patties (Kotlet Rybny), and Fish Salad (Sałatka Rybna), made with a combination of fish, vegetables, and mayonnaise.

The importance of Fish and Seafood Delights in Polish Cuisine goes beyond their delicious flavors. They provide essential nutrients, including omega-3 fatty acids, vitamins, and minerals, which are beneficial for overall health. Moreover, fish and seafood have been part of Polish culinary traditions for centuries, representing the country's connection to its natural environment and cultural heritage.

Fish and Seafood Delights have a significant place in Polish Cuisine. Whether it's the smoked salmon, fisherman's soup, or the variety of seafood dishes, they bring unique flavors and nutritional value to the table. These dishes reflect Poland's geographical location, cultural heritage, and the importance of embracing nature's bounties in their rich culinary traditions.

3.3.1 Karp Po Żydowsku: Jewish-Style Carp

Karp Po Żydowsku, also known as Jewish-Style Carp, holds great importance in Polish cuisine. This traditional dish has a long history and is often prepared during festive occasions, especially during Christmas Eve and Easter.

The dish consists of carp, a freshwater fish abundant in Poland, cooked in a unique and flavorful manner. The preparation of Karp Po Żydowsku involves marinating the fish in a mixture of lemon juice and spices such as cloves, allspice, and bay leaves. The marinated fish is then coated in flour and pan-fried until golden brown.

One of the key reasons for the significance of Karp Po Żydowsku in Polish cuisine is its association with cultural and religious traditions. In Poland, Christmas Eve is a special and sacred time for families to gather and celebrate. The traditional twelve-course meal, known as Wigilia, takes center stage during this celebration, and Karp Po Żydowsku is often the highlight of the meal. It symbolizes abundance, prosperity, and good luck for the upcoming year.

Beyond its cultural importance, Karp Po Żydowsku is also highly regarded for its delicious taste and unique flavor profile. The marinade infuses the fish with a tangy, aromatic essence that complements the tender and delicate flesh of the carp. The crispy outer layer adds a delightful texture to the dish. When combined with traditional side dishes like boiled potatoes and fresh vegetables, Karp Po Żydowsku creates a harmonious culinary experience.

Furthermore, Karp Po Żydowsku showcases the culinary creativity and resourcefulness of Polish cooks. The dish originated during a time when meat was not consumed on Christmas Eve due to religious observances. As a result, fish became a popular alternative, with carp gaining prominence due to its availability in Polish waters. The inventive methods of marinating and frying the fish reflect the ingenuity of Polish cooks in transforming simple ingredients into a memorable and flavorful dish.

Karp Po Żydowsku: Jewish-Style Carp holds immense importance in Polish cuisine due to its cultural, religious, and culinary significance. This dish not only symbolizes tradition and abundance but also highlights the culinary creativity and resourcefulness of Polish cooks. With its unique flavors and textures, Karp Po Żydowsku continues to be a beloved and iconic part of Polish festive celebrations.

3.3.2 Łosoś z Sosem Koperkowym: Salmon with Dill Sauce

Łosoś z Sosem Koperkowym, also known as Salmon with Dill Sauce, holds a significant place in Polish cuisine. This delectable dish showcases the rich culinary heritage and traditional flavors of Poland.

Salmon has long been a popular choice of fish in Poland due to its abundance in the Baltic Sea and freshwater rivers. It is highly regarded for its delicate texture and flavorful taste. When combined with the creamy and aromatic dill sauce, the result is a harmonious blend of flavors that tantalizes the taste buds.

The importance of Łosoś z Sosem Koperkowym in Polish cuisine can be attributed to several factors. Firstly, it represents the cultural heritage and pride of the Polish people. The use of local ingredients, such as fresh salmon and dill, highlights the connection to the land and the sea. It symbolizes the reliance on nature's bounty and the appreciation for traditional cooking methods.

Furthermore, Łosoś z Sosem Koperkowym is often prepared for special occasions and family gatherings. It is a dish that brings people together, fostering a sense of unity and celebration. Whether it's a wedding, Christmas dinner, or Easter feast, this dish is a beloved staple on Polish tables, creating cherished memories and strengthening familial bonds.

From a gastronomic perspective, Łosoś z Sosem Koperkowym showcases the skill and expertise of Polish chefs. The delicate balance of flavors in the dill sauce, complementing the succulent salmon, requires precision and knowledge of culinary techniques. This dish often represents the pinnacle of Polish cuisine, demonstrating the mastery of flavor profiles and the art of presentation.

In addition to its cultural and gastronomic significance, Łosoś z Sosem Koperkowym offers numerous health benefits. Salmon is known for its high omega-3 fatty acid content, which promotes heart health and reduces inflammation. Dill, a herb commonly used in the sauce, is a rich source of vitamins and minerals, aiding in digestion and boosting the immune system. Therefore, consuming this dish not only satisfies the palate but also contributes to overall well-being.

Łosoś z Sosem Koperkowym: Salmon with Dill Sauce holds great importance in Polish cuisine. It is a dish that reflects Polish traditions, brings people together, showcases culinary expertise, and offers health benefits. Whether enjoyed at a festive gathering or in a local restaurant, this dish is a testament to the rich culinary heritage and the enduring love for delicious food in Poland.

Chapter 4.Side Dishes and Accompaniments

The importance of Side Dishes and Accompaniments in Polish Cuisine cannot be overstated. These components play a crucial role in enhancing the overall dining experience by adding flavor, texture, and variety to the main course.

One of the most recognizable side dishes in Polish cuisine is kluski, which are small dumplings made from potatoes, flour, or both. Kluski can be boiled, fried, or baked, and they are commonly served alongside meat dishes or in soups. These little pillows of deliciousness bring a comforting element to the meal and provide a satisfying alternative to plain rice or bread.

Another staple side dish is kapusta, or sauerkraut. This fermented cabbage is not only packed with vitamins and minerals but also adds a tangy and slightly sour flavor to the meal. Sauerkraut is often served with meat, such as pierogi (stuffed dumplings) or bigos (hunter's stew). Its distinctive taste cuts through the richness of the main dish, making each bite more enjoyable.

Accompaniments like pickles are also widely loved in Polish cuisine. Whether it's dill pickles, cucumbers, or mixed vegetables, pickles add a burst of acidity and crunch to complement the flavors of meaty dishes. They can be enjoyed on their own or used as a condiment in sandwiches and salads.

Potato-based accompaniments are immensely popular in Poland. One such classic is placki ziemniaczane, also known as potato pancakes. These savory delights are made by grating potatoes, mixing them with eggs and flour, and frying them until golden brown. Potato pancakes are commonly served with sour cream or applesauce, and they make a delightful side dish or a delicious snack.

Side dishes and accompaniments in Polish cuisine are not limited to just these examples. Each region in Poland has its own specialties, ranging from creamy beetroot salad to hearty buckwheat groats. The variety in side dishes and accompaniments is a testament to the rich culinary traditions of Poland.

Side dishes and accompaniments are an essential part of Polish cuisine. They bring balance, flavor, and excitement to the table, elevating the main course and making it a complete and satisfying meal. So, the next time you enjoy a Polish feast, don't forget to savor the side dishes and accompaniments that make it truly special.

5.1 Comforting Potatoes

Comforting Potatoes play a significant role in the Polish Cuisine. They are a staple ingredient in many traditional Polish dishes and are cherished for their comforting and satisfying qualities.

One of the most well-known Polish potato dishes is "placki ziemniaczane" or potato pancakes. These delicious pancakes are made by grating potatoes and mixing them with flour, eggs, and various seasonings. They are then pan-fried until golden brown and served hot. Potato pancakes are often enjoyed with sour cream or applesauce. They are loved for their crispy texture on the outside and soft, fluffy interior.

Another popular Polish potato dish is "pyra z gzikiem," which translates to "potatoes with quark." This simple yet flavorful dish consists of boiled potatoes served with a creamy, tangy sauce made from quark cheese, garlic, and herbs. The combination of the creamy sauce and tender potatoes creates a delightful and comforting taste.

Potato dumplings, known as "kopytka," are another beloved Polish dish. These dumplings are made by combining mashed potatoes with flour and forming them into small, oval-shaped pieces. They are boiled until they become tender and are then usually served with a rich sauce or gravy. Kopytka are a comforting and filling dish that is perfect for chilly days.

Lastly, "ziemniaki zasmażane" or fried potatoes are commonly enjoyed in Polish cuisine. Thinly sliced potatoes are fried until golden and crispy, often with the addition of onions and bacon. This dish is versatile and can be served as a side dish or as a main course with added toppings like fried eggs or sausages. The combination of crispy potatoes and savory flavors makes it incredibly satisfying.

Comforting Potatoes hold a special place in Polish cuisine. Whether in the form of potato pancakes, potatoes with quark, potato dumplings, or fried potatoes, they add depth and flavor to traditional Polish dishes. The comforting and satisfying qualities of potatoes make them an essential ingredient in Polish culinary traditions.

5.1.1 Placki Ziemniaczane: Potato Pancakes

Potato pancakes, known as Placki Ziemniaczane, hold a significant place in Polish cuisine. These delectable and versatile delights have been cherished by generations and have become an essential part of Polish culinary traditions.

Placki Ziemniaczane are made using grated potatoes that are mixed with flour, eggs, and various seasonings. Traditional recipes also include finely chopped onions, which add a delightful flavor to the pancakes. The mixture is then fried until golden brown, resulting in crispy pancakes with a soft and fluffy interior.

One of the reasons why Placki Ziemniaczane are so important in Polish cuisine is their historical significance. Potatoes were introduced to Poland in the late 17th century, and they quickly became a staple food. Potato pancakes were an economical and filling dish that made use of the abundant potato crop. They provided sustenance to the Polish people during challenging times, such as wars and economic hardships.

Beyond their historical importance, Placki Ziemniaczane have also become a beloved comfort food in Poland. They are often enjoyed as a main course, served with a dollop of sour cream or applesauce. The crispy texture of the pancakes contrasts perfectly with the creamy toppings, creating a delightful culinary experience.

Furthermore, Placki Ziemniaczane can be served in various ways, making them incredibly versatile. They can be enjoyed simply with a sprinkle of salt, or they can be topped with savory additions such as bacon bits, cheese, or mushrooms. In some regions of Poland, Placki Ziemniaczane are even served as a dessert, drizzled with honey or sprinkled with powdered sugar.

Potato pancakes hold a special place in Polish culture and are often served during important festivities and family gatherings. They symbolize warmth, comfort, and togetherness, creating a sense of nostalgia and connection to Polish heritage.

Placki Ziemniaczane, or potato pancakes, are an integral part of Polish cuisine. Their historical significance, versatility, and comforting nature make them a beloved dish that continues to bring joy and satisfaction to those who partake in the Polish culinary experience. Whether enjoyed with traditional toppings or prepared with a modern twist, Placki Ziemniaczane are a true delight that celebrate the rich culinary heritage of Poland.

5.1.2 Pyzy: Potato Dumplings

Pyzy: Potato Dumplings play a significant role in Polish cuisine. These traditional Polish dumplings are made using simple ingredients such as mashed potatoes, flour, and sometimes eggs. The process of making pyzy involves shaping the dough into small balls and boiling them until they are fully cooked.

One of the key reasons why pyzy are important in Polish cuisine is their versatility. They can be served as a main dish, a side dish, or even as a part of soups. Pyzy can be served with a variety of toppings and accompaniments, such as fried onions, bacon bits, or a dollop of sour cream. This flexibility allows them to be incorporated into various meals and enjoyed by people of different taste preferences.

Another reason for the importance of pyzy in Polish cuisine is their cultural significance. These dumplings are deeply rooted in Polish culinary traditions and are often associated with special occasions and family gatherings. Pyzy are commonly served during holidays like Christmas and Easter, where families come together to celebrate and share a meal. The process of making pyzy can also be a communal activity, where family members gather in the kitchen to prepare the dough and shape the dumplings together.

Pyzy also represent a sense of comfort and familiarity in Polish cuisine. The soft texture of the dumplings, combined with the flavors of potatoes, creates a satisfying and hearty meal. They evoke a sense of nostalgia and remind people of home-cooked meals from their childhood. Whether served with savory or sweet toppings, pyzy provide a sense of comfort and familiarity that is deeply cherished in Polish culinary culture.

Additionally, pyzy are a representation of the resourcefulness of Polish cuisine. Potatoes have been a staple crop in Poland for centuries, and pyzy have emerged as a delicious and practical way to utilize this ingredient. By combining potatoes and flour, pyzy offer a filling and economical meal option. They showcase the ability of Polish cuisine to create flavorful dishes using simple and readily available ingredients.

Pyzy: Potato Dumplings hold great significance in Polish cuisine. Their versatility, cultural importance, comfort factor, and resourcefulness all contribute to their popularity. Whether served as a main course or accompanying dish, pyzy are beloved by the Polish people and offer a delightful culinary experience.

5.2 The Sauerkraut Connection

The Sauerkraut Connection plays a significant role in Polish cuisine. Sauerkraut, also known as fermented cabbage, is a staple ingredient in many traditional Polish dishes. It is made by fermenting cabbage with salt, which results in a tangy and slightly sour flavor. The process of fermentation not only enhances the taste of the cabbage but also provides numerous health benefits.

One of the main reasons for the importance of the Sauerkraut Connection is its role in preserving food. Historically, sauerkraut was crucial in extending the shelf life of vegetables during long, harsh Polish winters. The fermentation process involved in making sauerkraut helps preserve the cabbage for extended periods without the need for refrigeration. This was particularly valuable in times when fresh produce was scarce.

Aside from its preservation properties, sauerkraut is also rich in probiotics. These are beneficial bacteria that promote a healthy gut flora. Consuming sauerkraut can contribute to improved digestion and overall gut health. Furthermore, probiotics are believed to strengthen the immune system and may even have positive effects on mental health.

The Sauerkraut Connection is deeply embedded in Polish culinary traditions. It is a key ingredient in iconic Polish dishes like bigos, which is a hearty sauerkraut and meat stew, and pierogi, where sauerkraut serves as a flavorful filling. Polish cuisine, with its emphasis on comfort food and hearty flavors, often incorporates sauerkraut as a way to add depth and tanginess to the dishes.

Moreover, sauerkraut is a versatile ingredient that can be enjoyed in various forms. Whether it's used as a condiment, a side dish, or a main ingredient, sauerkraut adds a unique and distinct flavor to many Polish recipes. Its tangy taste provides a refreshing contrast to the richness of meats and other ingredients.

The Sauerkraut Connection is of great importance in Polish cuisine. Its role in food preservation, health benefits, and contribution to traditional recipes makes it an essential ingredient in many Polish dishes. The tangy, sour flavor of sauerkraut adds a unique element to the overall taste profile of Polish cuisine, making it beloved by locals and appreciated by food enthusiasts worldwide.

5.2.1 Kapusniak: Cabbage Soup

The Kapusniak, or Cabbage Soup, holds great significance in Polish cuisine. It is a traditional dish that reflects the rich culinary heritage of Poland. This soup has been enjoyed by generations and continues to be a beloved comfort food in the country.

One of the reasons why Kapusniak is important in Polish cuisine is its historical significance. Cabbage has been cultivated in Poland for centuries, and cabbage-based soups have been a part of the Polish diet since ancient times. Cabbage was a staple vegetable that could be easily grown and preserved, making it an essential ingredient in Polish cooking. The Kapusniak originated as a way to make use of the abundance of cabbage, especially during the winter months when fresh vegetables were scarce.

Besides its historical importance, the Kapusniak also represents the Polish culture and culinary traditions. It showcases the use of simple, yet flavorful ingredients that are commonly found in Polish households. The soup typically includes sauerkraut, which adds a tangy and sour flavor, along with other vegetables like onions, carrots, and potatoes. It is often seasoned with herbs and spices like bay leaves, peppercorns, and marjoram, enhancing the taste and aroma of the soup.

The Kapusniak is not only a delicious dish but also offers important nutritional benefits. Cabbage is a cruciferous vegetable that is rich in vitamins, minerals, and dietary fiber. It is known for its antioxidant properties and may even have potential health benefits, such as reducing the risk of certain diseases. Additionally, the soup is usually a hearty and filling meal, providing warmth and comfort during colder days.

In Polish culture, the Kapusniak holds a special place during events and celebrations. It is often served during festive occasions, such as weddings, Christmas, and Easter. Sharing a bowl of Kapusniak with family and friends symbolizes togetherness, unity, and the appreciation of Polish culinary traditions.

The Kapusniak: Cabbage Soup is not only a staple in Polish cuisine but also a cultural symbol and a testament to the country's culinary heritage. Its historical significance, simplicity, nutritional value, and role in celebrations contribute to its importance in Polish culinary traditions. Whether enjoyed on a cold winter day or shared with loved ones during special occasions, the Kapusniak continues to remind Polish people of their roots and the flavors that have shaped their culture for centuries.

5.2.2 Kielbasa z Kapustą: Sausage with Sauerkraut

Kielbasa z Kapustą, commonly known as Sausage with Sauerkraut, is a classic Polish dish that holds significant importance in Polish cuisine. This flavorful and hearty dish reflects the deep-rooted traditions and cultural heritage of Poland.

One of the key reasons why Kielbasa z Kapustą is highly valued in Polish cuisine is its rich taste and aroma. The combination of savory sausage and tangy sauerkraut creates a unique and satisfying flavor profile. The sauerkraut, made from fermented cabbage, adds a refreshing and slightly sour taste, complementing the savory and juicy sausage perfectly.

Beyond its delicious taste, Kielbasa z Kapustą also has a historical significance in Polish culture. Sausage-making has been a part of Polish culinary tradition for centuries. The art of preserving meat by smoking and curing was essential in the past to ensure a stable food supply during harsh winters. Sausages were a staple in Polish households, and Kielbasa z Kapustą emerged as a popular dish among both the nobility and commoners.

The dish also showcases the use of locally available ingredients, reflecting the importance of seasonality and sustainability in Polish cuisine. Cabbage, a common vegetable in Poland, is abundant during colder months and can be preserved as sauerkraut throughout the year. Along with sausage, which can be made from a variety of meats, Kielbasa z Kapustą embodies the principle of using fresh and easily accessible ingredients.

Furthermore, Kielbasa z Kapustą holds a special place in Polish festivals and celebrations. It is often served during Christmas Eve and Easter, as well as on other important occasions like weddings and family gatherings. The dish symbolizes unity, tradition, and sharing meals with loved ones, reinforcing the importance of community and togetherness in Polish culture.

Kielbasa z Kapustą: Sausage with Sauerkraut is an integral part of Polish cuisine, representing the country's culinary traditions, historical significance, and cultural values. Its delicious flavor, locally sourced ingredients, and role in festive celebrations make it a cherished dish among the Polish people. Whether enjoyed at family dinners or served during special occasions, Kielbasa z Kapustą showcases the essence and importance of Polish culinary heritage.

Chapter 5. Polish Desserts and Sweets

Polish Desserts and Sweets play a significant role in the Polish Cuisine. These delectable treats are not only enjoyed on special occasions but are also an integral part of everyday Polish life.

One of the most iconic Polish desserts is the Polish Apple Pie, also known as Szarlotka. Made with a buttery crust and filled with sweet and tart apples, it is a perfect balance of flavors. It is commonly served with a dollop of whipped cream or a scoop of vanilla ice cream. The Polish Apple Pie represents the simplicity and elegance of Polish cuisine.

Another popular Polish dessert is the Paczki, a deep-fried pastry filled with various sweet fillings such as jam, custard, or chocolate. Traditionally, Paczki are enjoyed on Fat Thursday, which is the last Thursday before Lent. These delightful pastries are symbolically consumed before the fasting period begins.

Polish Babka is a traditional yeast cake that is often served during Easter celebrations. It is made with rich ingredients like butter, eggs, and yeast, giving it a soft and fluffy texture. Babka can be flavored with various ingredients such as raisins, almonds, or chocolate. It is enjoyed with a cup of tea or coffee, making it a perfect treat for social gatherings.

An essential Polish sweet is the Kołaczki, a bite-sized pastry filled with fruit preserves, nuts, or cheese. These delicate pastries are a staple during Christmas festivities. Kołaczki are often dusted with powdered sugar, adding a touch of elegance to the dessert.

The Polish cuisine also boasts a wide variety of cookies and cakes. Makowiec, a poppy seed roll, is a popular dessert during Christmas and Easter. Kremówka, also known as Napoleons, is a layered pastry filled with thick vanilla custard, and it is a true indulgence for any dessert lover.

Polish desserts and sweets bring people together, offering a sweet ending to any meal or celebration. Their rich flavors, intricate textures, and cultural significance make them an integral part of the Polish culinary tradition. From simple apple pies to elaborate cakes, Polish desserts are a testament to the country's love for good food and heartfelt hospitality.

6.1 Decadent Cakes and Pastries

Decadent Cakes and Pastries hold great importance in Polish cuisine. These indulgent treats are not only delicious but also have cultural significance in the country's culinary traditions.

One of the iconic Polish desserts is the famous Polish Cheesecake, known as "Sernik." Made with cream cheese, eggs, sugar, and various flavorings such as vanilla or lemon zest, Sernik has a smooth and creamy texture that melts in your mouth. It is often served with a dusting of powdered sugar or a dollop of whipped cream. Sernik is a beloved dessert that is enjoyed during holidays and family gatherings, and it represents the celebration and joy of Polish cuisine.

Another staple in Polish pastry is the "Pączki." These deep-fried doughnuts are usually filled with raspberry or rose jam, but modern variations can include vanilla or chocolate cream. Pączki are traditionally consumed on Fat Thursday, which precedes Lent. These sweet treats are symbolic of indulgence and abundance before the fasting period begins.

A classic Polish cake that cannot be overlooked is the "Babka." This rich and moist yeast-based cake is often baked in a distinctive fluted pan. Babka is typically flavored with vanilla, lemon zest, or rum, and sometimes filled with chocolate or raisins. It is commonly served during Easter and Christmas celebrations, symbolizing the joy and festivity of these occasions.

In addition to these specific desserts, Poland boasts a wide range of other decadent cakes and pastries, such as "Makowiec" (poppy seed roll), "Kremówka" (cream cake), and "Napoleonka" (Napoleon cake). Each of these delicacies has its own unique preparation method and taste, adding diversity to the Polish dessert repertoire.

Decadent cakes and pastries in Polish cuisine not only satisfy the sweet tooth but also reflect the Polish people's dedication to culinary artistry and tradition. These desserts have been cherished for generations, passed down through families, and incorporated into festive occasions. They are a testament to Poland's rich gastronomic heritage and the love for indulgent treats that bring people together.

6.1.1 Sernik: Polish Cheesecake

Sernik, also known as Polish cheesecake, holds great importance in the Polish cuisine. It is a traditional dessert that has been enjoyed by generations and plays a significant role in Polish culinary traditions.

Sernik has a rich history dating back to medieval times, where it was originally prepared by Catholic monks in monasteries. The recipe has been passed down through generations, and it has become a staple dessert in Polish households.

The main ingredient of Sernik is twaróg, a type of Polish curd cheese. Twaróg is known for its creamy texture and tangy flavor, which gives the cheesecake its distinct taste. Other common ingredients include eggs, sugar, and often a hint of vanilla or lemon zest to enhance the flavor profile.

Polish cheesecake is known for its dense and moist texture, setting it apart from other varieties of cheesecake. It is often baked in a round or square shape, and the top is typically adorned with a mixture of either traditional crumble, fruits, or a sweet glaze.

Sernik is not only popular for its delectable taste but also holds cultural significance. It is often served during holidays and celebrations, such as Easter and Christmas. Families gather around the table to enjoy a slice of Sernik, creating lasting memories and upholding Polish traditions.

The popularity of Sernik extends beyond Poland's borders, as it has gained recognition internationally. Polish communities around the world continue to preserve their culinary heritage by preparing Sernik for various occasions.

Sernik, Polish cheesecake, is a beloved dessert that holds great importance in Polish cuisine. Its rich history, unique texture, and cultural significance make it a cherished part of Polish culinary traditions. Whether enjoyed during festive gatherings or simply as a sweet treat, Sernik continues to bring joy and unite people through its deliciousness.

6.1.2 Napoleonka: Polish Custard Slice

Napoleonka: Polish Custard Slice is a beloved dessert in Polish cuisine. It is a rich and indulgent pastry that holds great importance in Polish culinary traditions.

The Napoleonka consists of layers of flaky puff pastry filled with a luscious custard cream. The pastry is baked to perfection, resulting in a golden and crisp exterior that contrasts beautifully with the smooth and creamy filling. The custard is typically made with ingredients such as eggs, milk, sugar, and vanilla, which give it a rich and comforting flavor.

This delectable dessert has a long history in Poland and has become a staple in many Polish households and bakeries. It is often enjoyed on special occasions, such as birthdays, holidays, or family gatherings. Its popularity can be attributed to its delicious taste and the warm memories it evokes.

The significance of Napoleonka in Polish cuisine goes beyond its exquisite flavor. It holds cultural and sentimental value for many Poles. It is a dessert that has been passed down through generations, with recipes being handed down from mothers to daughters. The process of making Napoleonka is often a family affair, bringing loved ones together and creating a sense of tradition and togetherness.

Moreover, Napoleonka represents Polish pastry craftsmanship at its finest. The delicate layers of puff pastry require skill and precision to achieve the perfect balance of crispness and tenderness. The custard filling, with its smooth texture and subtle sweetness, showcases the artistry of Polish bakers.

In addition, Napoleonka has gained recognition internationally, drawing interest from pastry enthusiasts and food lovers around the world. It serves as a delightful ambassador for Polish cuisine, showcasing the country's culinary prowess.

Ultimately, Napoleonka: Polish Custard Slice holds immense importance in Polish cuisine for its delectable taste, cultural significance, and representation of Polish pastry tradition. Whether enjoyed during special occasions or as a simple pleasure, this dessert continues to bring joy and satisfaction to those who indulge in its creamy decadence.

6.2 Sweet Comforts

Sweet comforts play a significant role in Polish cuisine. They are not only a source of pleasure but also a way to connect with Polish culture and traditions. Polish sweets are known for their unique flavors, rich textures, and beautiful presentation.

One popular sweet comfort in Polish cuisine is the piernik, also known as gingerbread. Piernik is a spiced honey cake that has been enjoyed in Poland for centuries. It is often made with a combination of honey, flour, eggs, and various spices such as cinnamon, cloves, and nutmeg. Piernik is usually dense and moist, and it can be enjoyed plain or with a coating of chocolate or icing.

Another beloved sweet comfort in Poland is the paczki. Paczki are deep-fried donuts that are traditionally filled with sweet fillings such as jam or custard. They are typically eaten on Fat Thursday, which is the last Thursday before Lent. Paczki are enjoyed by people of all ages and are a symbol of indulgence before the fasting period of Lent begins.

Krówka, also known as a milk caramel, is another popular sweet in Polish cuisine. It is made by simmering sweetened condensed milk until it reaches a thick and creamy consistency. Krówka is often wrapped in wax paper and enjoyed as a small treat. It has a rich and indulgent taste, making it a perfect accompaniment to a cup of coffee or tea.

Sweet comforts also hold cultural significance in Poland. They are often enjoyed during holidays and celebrations, such as Christmas and Easter. Polish families have passed down recipes for generations, making sweets a way to connect with their heritage and create lasting memories.

Sweet comforts are an integral part of Polish cuisine. From traditional gingerbread and paczki to milk caramels, these sweets bring joy and cultural significance. They not only satisfy the taste buds but also provide an opportunity to celebrate Polish traditions and create meaningful connections.

6.2.1 Pączki: Polish Doughnuts

Pączki, also known as Polish doughnuts, hold significant importance in Polish cuisine. These delicious pastries have a long history and have become a staple in Polish culture.

One of the main reasons why pączki are important in Polish cuisine is their deep-rooted tradition. They are traditionally made and enjoyed on Fat Thursday, which falls before the Catholic season of Lent. This day is highly anticipated in Poland, and families and friends gather to indulge in these sweet treats. The tradition of making and enjoying pączki has been passed down through generations, adding to its cultural significance.

Pączki are also beloved for their unique and flavorsome taste. These doughnuts are typically filled with various sweet fillings, such as plum jam, rose petal jam, or custard. The soft and fluffy dough, combined with the luscious filling, creates a delightful explosion of flavors. The pleasure of biting into a freshly made pączek is unparalleled and leaves a lasting impression on anyone who tries it.

In addition to their taste, pączki hold a symbolic meaning in Polish culture. They are often associated with good luck and prosperity. The round shape of the doughnuts symbolizes the circle of life and the hope for a prosperous year ahead. It is believed that consuming pączki on Fat Thursday brings good fortune, making them an essential part of Polish celebrations.

Furthermore, the process of making pączki requires skill and dedication. Traditional recipes require the dough to be made from scratch using high-quality ingredients such as flour, eggs, milk, and yeast. The dough is then hand-formed into small rounds, fried until golden brown, and generously filled with a delectable filling. This craftsmanship and attention to detail make pączki a cherished culinary art form in Polish cuisine.

Beyond their cultural and symbolic importance, pączki have gained international recognition and popularity. Polish communities around the world celebrate Fat Thursday by making and sharing these delightful treats, spreading the joy and appreciation for Polish cuisine. Pączki have even been embraced by people from different backgrounds who have come to appreciate their unique flavors and cultural significance.

Pączki are more than just doughnuts in Polish cuisine. They embody tradition, cultural identity, and culinary artistry. The combination of their delicious taste, symbolic meaning, and international recognition makes pączki an essential part of Polish cuisine and a beloved treat for people around the world.

6.2.2 Makowiec: Poppy Seed Roll

Makowiec, also known as Poppy Seed Roll, holds a significant place in Polish cuisine. This traditional pastry is deeply rooted in Polish culinary heritage and is widely celebrated throughout the country.

One of the key reasons for the importance of Makowiec in Polish cuisine is its historical significance. Dating back to the 17th century, Makowiec has been a staple dessert during Christmas and Easter celebrations. Its presence on festive tables symbolizes joy, abundance, and tradition. The preparation and consumption of Makowiec have been passed down through generations, making it a cherished part of Polish culture.

The uniqueness of Makowiec lies in its exquisite flavor profile. The filling is made with ground poppy seeds, which are blended with sugar, honey, and sometimes nuts or dried fruits. The mixture is then spread onto a yeast-based dough, rolled up, and baked to golden perfection. The resulting Poppy Seed Roll is a delightful combination of nutty, sweet, and slightly tangy flavors. Its dense and moist texture adds an indulgent element to every bite.

Apart from its delicious taste, Makowiec is also associated with various symbolic meanings. In Polish folklore, poppy seeds are believed to bring good luck and fertility. Therefore, serving Makowiec during festive occasions is considered a wish for prosperity and well-being. Moreover, the poppy seeds used in Makowiec are rich in essential nutrients like calcium, iron, and omega-3 fatty acids. This makes the pastry not only a treat for the taste buds but also a wholesome dessert choice.

Makowiec is not limited to special occasions but is also enjoyed as an everyday treat in Poland. It can be found in bakeries, pastry shops, and even homemade with love. The popularity of Makowiec extends beyond Poland's borders as well, with Polish communities worldwide cherishing this traditional pastry and keeping their culinary heritage alive.

Makowiec holds great importance in Polish cuisine due to its historical significance, unique flavor profile, and symbolic associations. Its presence on festive tables and everyday indulgence showcases its place as a beloved dessert that embodies tradition, celebration, and the richness of Polish culinary heritage.

Chapter 6. Regional Delicacies

Regional delicacies play a vital role in Polish cuisine, adding diversity and uniqueness to the culinary traditions of different regions. These local specialties showcase the rich cultural heritage and historical influences that have shaped Polish gastronomy over the centuries.

One prominent regional delicacy is the pierogi, a type of dumpling that can be found in various fillings and flavors across Poland. Each region has its own twist on this popular dish, such as the Ruskie pierogi with potato and cheese filling in the Podlasie region, or the sweet fruit-filled pierogi commonly enjoyed in the Podhale region.

Another notable regional delicacy is oscypek, a smoked cheese made from sheep's milk. This cheese, typically found in the Tatra Mountains region, has a distinct shape and flavor that is loved by locals and tourists alike. It is often served grilled with cranberry sauce, providing a delightful combination of savory and sweet.

In the Kashubia region, the kaszanka is a beloved local delicacy. This blood sausage is made from a mixture of pork meat, buckwheat or barley, and pig's blood. It is traditionally seasoned with marjoram, garlic, and other herbs, giving it a unique and flavorful taste. Kaszanka is often fried or grilled and served as a main course.

Moving to the seaside, the Baltic herring, known as śledź, is a significant part of the culinary heritage in the coastal regions. Whether pickled, smoked, or fried, this fish is a staple ingredient in many traditional dishes. It is often served as a main course, in salads, or as an appetizer with bread and butter.

These are just a few examples of the regional delicacies that make Polish cuisine so diverse and fascinating. Each dish reflects the local traditions, ingredients, and cultural influences of its respective region. The importance of regional delicacies lies in their ability to preserve and showcase the unique flavors and culinary heritage of different parts of Poland. Exploring these delicacies allows us to appreciate the diversity within Polish cuisine and the rich tapestry of flavors that define the country's gastronomy.

7.1 Tastes of Different Regions

Polish cuisine is known for its rich and diverse flavors, which vary across different regions of the country. Each region in Poland has its own unique culinary traditions and preferences, resulting in a fascinating tapestry of tastes that reflect the country's history, geography, and cultural heritage.

One of the regions that stands out in terms of taste is Mazovia, where the capital city, Warsaw, is located. Mazovian cuisine is characterized by its hearty and rustic flavors. Traditional dishes like bigos (hunter's stew), pierogi (dumplings), and żurek (sour rye soup) are staple foods in this region. The taste of Mazovian cuisine is often described as robust, with a blend of smoky, sour, and savory flavors that leave a lasting impression.

Moving to the north of Poland, the Baltic Sea coast brings a distinct flavor profile to the Polish cuisine. Fresh seafood, particularly Baltic herring and cod, is widely enjoyed in this region. The taste of the ocean is subtly reflected in dishes such as fish soup and smoked fish, which are popular coastal delicacies. Additionally, the coastal region is known for its amber honey and wild mushroom dishes, which add depth and earthiness to the local cuisine.

Venturing to the south of Poland, we find the mountainous region of Podhale, home to the picturesque Tatra Mountains. In this region, traditional highlander cuisine, known as "góralska kuchnia," takes center stage. The taste of Podhale is characterized by bold and spicy flavors, with dishes like oscypek (smoked cheese), kwaśnica (sauerkraut soup), and kwaśnica z kapustą (sauerkraut with cabbage) being popular choices. The use of local herbs and spices, such as juniper berries and marjoram, adds a distinct aroma and taste to the cuisine.

Lastly, we cannot overlook the Wielkopolska region in central-western Poland. Known for its abundant farmland, this region boasts a cuisine that highlights the freshness and quality of its produce. Classic dishes like pyra z gzikiem (potatoes with cottage cheese), flaki (tripe soup), and rogal świętomarciński (St. Martin's croissant) are cherished in Wielkopolska. The taste of this region is characterized by simplicity and the natural flavors of ingredients, resulting in a satisfying and wholesome culinary experience.

The importance of the tastes of different regions in the Polish cuisine cannot be overstated. They not only showcase the diversity and cultural richness of Poland but also serve as a testament to the country's historical and geographical influences. Exploring the distinct flavors of Mazovia, the Baltic Sea coast, Podhale, and Wielkopolska allows us to appreciate the true essence of Polish cuisine and its regional variations. So, when it comes to exploring Polish flavors, be sure to embark on a culinary journey across the different regions of this fascinating country.

7.1.1 Silesian Streuselkuchen

Silesian Streuselkuchen, also known as Silesian Butter Cake, holds great importance in Polish cuisine. This traditional German pastry has become an integral part of Polish culinary heritage, enjoyed by people of all ages.

The significance of Silesian Streuselkuchen can be attributed to its rich history and delectable taste. It originated in the Silesia region, which is now divided between Poland, Germany, and the Czech Republic. The cake was introduced to Polish cuisine during the centuries of German settlements in Silesia. Over time, it gained popularity and became a beloved dessert in Poland.

The distinctiveness of Silesian Streuselkuchen lies in its soft yeast dough and buttery crumble topping. The dough is made by combining flour, yeast, sugar, eggs, milk, and butter, resulting in a tender and fluffy base. The crumble topping, consisting of flour, sugar, and butter, adds a delightful crispness and enhances the cake's flavor.

One of the reasons for the cake's importance is its association with special occasions and celebrations. Silesian Streuselkuchen is commonly served during holidays, such as Christmas and Easter, as well as family gatherings and birthdays. Its presence on these joyful occasions symbolizes tradition, togetherness, and festivity.

Another aspect that contributes to its significance is the nostalgia it evokes. Many Poles have fond childhood memories of enjoying Silesian Streuselkuchen, often made by their grandparents or parents. The cake's aroma fills the kitchen, creating an atmosphere of warmth and comfort. It holds a sentimental value, reminding people of cherished moments and fostering a sense of belonging.

Moreover, Silesian Streuselkuchen reflects the cultural exchange and fusion within Polish cuisine. As the cake originated from German settlements, it represents the historical connection between Poland and Germany. It exemplifies how culinary traditions can intertwine and evolve, shaping the gastronomic identity of a nation.

In recent years, Silesian Streuselkuchen has gained international recognition, attracting tourists and food enthusiasts from around the world. Its unique texture, tantalizing appearance, and tantalizing taste have made it a sought-after treat. Polish bakeries and patisseries proudly showcase this delicacy, emphasizing its cultural significance.

To conclude, Silesian Streuselkuchen holds great importance in Polish cuisine due to its historical significance, nostalgic value, and representation of cultural fusion. This delightful pastry has become a beloved symbol of tradition, celebration, and unity. Its presence on festive occasions and in the culinary landscape of Poland is a testament to its enduring significance.

7.1.2 Podpłomyki: Polish Pancakes

Podpłomyki, also known as Polish Pancakes, hold a significant place in Polish cuisine. These traditional pancakes are not just a delightful treat but also carry cultural and historical importance. They have been an integral part of Polish culinary heritage for centuries.

One of the main reasons why Podpłomyki are important in Polish cuisine is their versatility. These pancakes can be enjoyed in various ways, making them suitable for different occasions. Whether they are served as a sweet dessert topped with fruits or as a savory dish filled with mushrooms and cheese, Podpłomyki offer a wide range of flavors to suit different tastes.

Furthermore, Podpłomyki represent the connection between the past and the present. The recipe for these pancakes has been passed down through generations, allowing the traditions and techniques to be preserved. By indulging in Podpłomyki, one can taste a bit of the history and tradition that has shaped Polish cuisine.

In addition to their cultural significance, Podpłomyki also showcase the abundance of local ingredients in Poland. The pancakes are typically made with simple ingredients such as flour, eggs, and milk, which are readily available. By using these basic ingredients, Polish cooks can create a dish that is both delicious and economical.

Podpłomyki also symbolize unity and togetherness within Polish families. Often prepared for special occasions such as weddings, birthdays, and holidays, these pancakes bring people together around the dining table. Sharing a plate of Podpłomyki fosters a sense of community and strengthens family ties, making them an important part of Polish culinary traditions.

Furthermore, Podpłomyki are not only enjoyed within Poland but have gained popularity around the world. Polish immigrants introduced these pancakes to various countries, allowing others to experience the unique flavors and cultural heritage they represent. This global recognition showcases the influence and impact of Polish cuisine beyond national borders.

Podpłomyki hold immense importance in Polish cuisine. They not only provide a delicious culinary experience but also represent cultural heritage, historical traditions, and the gathering of loved ones. With their versatility, simplicity, and ability to bring people together, Podpłomyki will continue to hold a cherished place in the hearts and plates of Polish people and those who appreciate the richness of their cuisine.

Chapter 7. Preserves, Pickles, and Condiments

Preserves, pickles, and condiments play a vital role in Polish cuisine. They not only enhance the flavors of various dishes but also contribute to the preservation of seasonal produce and create a diverse culinary experience.

Preserves, such as jams and fruit compotes, are widely used in Polish cuisine. They are made by cooking fruits or vegetables with sugar, resulting in a thick, sweet, and flavorful spread. Polish preserves showcase the abundance of fresh fruits, including berries, plums, apples, and cherries, during the harvest season. They are commonly enjoyed on bread, in desserts, or as a side accompaniment to savory dishes.

Pickles are another essential part of Polish cuisine. Traditional Polish pickles are made using cucumbers, cabbage, or other vegetables, along with a mixture of water, salt, herbs, and spices. These pickles are fermented, which not only gives them a unique tangy flavor but also increases their shelf life. Pickled cucumbers, known as ogórki kiszone, are particularly popular in Poland. They are often served as a side dish, added to sandwiches, or used as a key ingredient in many traditional Polish dishes, such as sour rye soup (żurek) or cucumber salad (mizeria).

Condiments, ranging from mustard and horseradish to various sauces, bring a burst of flavor to Polish dishes. Mustard (musztarda) is commonly used as a condiment to enhance the taste of sausages, cold cuts, and grilled meats. Horseradish (chrzan) is another popular condiment known for its sharp and pungent taste. It is often grated and mixed with vinegar or sour cream to create a creamy accompaniment for dishes such as roasted meats or beetroot soup (barszcz).

In addition to these specific examples, Polish cuisine utilizes a wide range of other preserves, pickles, and condiments to add complexity and depth to dishes. These include various fruit preserves, sauerkraut, pickled mushrooms, pickled beets, and tomato sauce, among others.

Preserves, pickles, and condiments are not only flavorful additions but also reflect the seasonality of Polish cuisine. They allow the enjoyment of the vibrant flavors of fruits and vegetables throughout the year while providing a delightful burst of taste in every bite. Whether it's the sweetness of preserves, the tanginess of pickles, or the boldness of condiments, these culinary elements have become an integral part of Polish cuisine, contributing to its rich and diverse gastronomy.

8.1 Homemade Goodies

The importance of Homemade Goodies in the Polish Cuisine is significant. Homemade goodies, also known as "ciasta domowe" in Polish, play a central role in traditional Polish culinary traditions. These homemade treats are not only delicious but also represent a form of cultural heritage.

One of the key reasons why Homemade Goodies hold importance in Polish cuisine is their connection to family traditions and celebrations. In Poland, it is common for families to gather and celebrate special occasions, such as birthdays, name days, holidays, and religious festivals. During these gatherings, homemade goodies take the spotlight and serve as a symbol of love, care, and tradition. Grandmothers, mothers, and even children continue the legacy of making these treats from scratch, passing down cherished recipes from generation to generation.

Moreover, Homemade Goodies in Polish cuisine showcase the country's diverse and rich culinary heritage. Poland is renowned for its wide variety of cakes, pastries, desserts, and cookies. Each region in Poland has its own unique specialties and traditional recipes. For example, the Mazurka cake from Mazovia, the Sękacz cake from Podlasie, and the Silesian gingerbread from Silesia are just a few examples of celebrated homemade goodies that represent the culinary identity of specific regions.

The use of high-quality ingredients is another crucial aspect of Homemade Goodies in Polish cuisine. The emphasis on using fresh, natural, and locally sourced ingredients sets these treats apart from their commercial counterparts. Traditional Polish recipes often call for ingredients like real butter, farm-fresh eggs, organic fruits, and nuts. This focus on quality creates homemade goodies that not only taste exceptional but also promote a healthier and more wholesome culinary experience.

Furthermore, Homemade Goodies allow for creative expression and innovation within Polish cuisine. Bakers and home cooks have the freedom to experiment with flavors, textures, and presentations. This artistic freedom leads to the creation of unique and personalized homemade treats. Polish cuisine enthusiasts are always in awe of the inventive combinations and delightful surprises that homemade goodies have to offer.

Lastly, Homemade Goodies in Polish cuisine contribute to the preservation of cultural identity. As Poland continues to evolve and embrace modern influences, the desire to maintain traditional culinary practices becomes even more vital. Homemade goodies act as a link between past and present, helping to keep Polish culture alive. They bring comfort, joy, and a sense of belonging to those who enjoy them, both within Poland and in Polish communities worldwide.

Homemade Goodies hold great importance in the Polish Cuisine. They represent family, tradition, diversity, quality, creativity, and cultural preservation. Whether it's a celebratory occasion or a simple gesture of love, homemade goodies bring people together and provide a taste of Poland's culinary heritage. So, next time you indulge in a Polish homemade treat, remember the significance it carries in preserving tradition and embracing the rich flavors of Polish cuisine.

8.1.1 Kisiel: Fruit Jelly Drink

Kisiel: Fruit Jelly Drink is a popular and significant component of Polish cuisine. This refreshing beverage has been enjoyed by generations and holds a special place in Polish culinary traditions.

One of the key reasons for the importance of Kisiel in Polish cuisine is its versatility. It can be made from various fruits, such as strawberries, raspberries, cherries, or plums, allowing for a wide range of flavors to be explored. The fruit is boiled with water and sweetened with sugar to create a thick, jelly-like consistency. This process not only enhances the natural sweetness of the fruit but also preserves its flavor and nutrients.

In Polish households, Kisiel is often made from seasonal fruits, making it a favorite treat during the summer months. Families gather together to harvest fruits from their gardens or visit local farmers' markets, creating a sense of community and connection to nature. Making Kisiel from scratch reinforces the value of using fresh, locally sourced ingredients in Polish cooking.

Kisiel can be served in various ways, depending on personal preference. Some enjoy it as a refreshing drink, while others enjoy it as a dessert by adding toppings such as whipped cream, fresh fruits, or even a sprinkle of powdered sugar. Its versatility allows it to be adapted to different occasions, whether it's a casual family gathering or a formal dinner party.

Beyond its delicious taste, Kisiel holds cultural significance in Polish cuisine. It has been a part of Polish culinary traditions for centuries, with recipes passed down through generations. Serving Kisiel is a way to honor and preserve Polish heritage, keeping traditions alive. It is often enjoyed during holiday celebrations, such as Christmas or Easter, bringing a sense of nostalgia and familial warmth to the table.

Kisiel: Fruit Jelly Drink plays a vital role in Polish cuisine. Its versatility, use of fresh ingredients, and cultural significance make it an essential part of Polish culinary traditions. Whether enjoyed as a refreshing drink or a delightful dessert, Kisiel brings people together and fosters a deep connection to Polish culture and heritage.

8.1.2 Kompot: Fruit Compote

Kompot, a fruit compote commonly found in Polish cuisine, holds great importance in the culinary tradition of Poland. With its unique flavors and refreshing qualities, kompot has become a staple beverage in Polish households and is often served during special occasions and celebrations.

One of the primary reasons why kompot is valued in Polish cuisine is its rich history. Dating back to the 17th century, kompot has been cherished as a way to preserve fruits and extend their shelf life. This was particularly important during the winter months when fresh fruits were scarce. By cooking a combination of fruits, such as apples, pears, berries, and cherries, with sugar and water, the fruits' flavors were extracted and preserved, creating a delicious and nutritious beverage that could be enjoyed throughout the year.

Furthermore, kompot is celebrated for its versatility. It can be prepared with a wide variety of fruits, allowing for countless flavor combinations. Whether it's a refreshing mix of summer berries or a comforting blend of autumn apples and plums, kompot can be tailored to suit individual preferences and seasonal produce. The flexibility of kompot not only appeals to the taste buds but also provides an opportunity to utilize surplus or overripe fruits, reducing food waste.

In addition to its taste and adaptability, kompot offers several health benefits. As a non-alcoholic beverage, it is suitable for all ages and is often served to children and adults alike. Kompot is packed with essential vitamins, minerals, and antioxidants derived from the fruits used in its preparation. These nutrients contribute to maintaining a healthy immune system, aiding digestion, and promoting overall wellness. Moreover, the natural sweetness of kompot, derived from the fruits themselves, makes it a healthier alternative to sugary soft drinks or artificial fruit juices.

In Polish culture, kompot holds a special place on the dining table. It is frequently served as a refreshing accompaniment to meals and is considered a symbol of hospitality. The act of preparing kompot, often involving family members and generations passing down recipes, fosters a sense of tradition and unity. Sharing a glass of kompot during family gatherings or festive occasions reinforces the communal spirit that is deeply ingrained in Polish culture.

The significance of kompot in Polish cuisine is undeniable. Its historical roots, versatility, health benefits, and cultural importance make it an integral part of Polish culinary heritage. As a beloved fruit compote, kompot represents the essence of Polish hospitality, tradition, and the appreciation of nature's bounty. So, the next time you have the opportunity, don't miss the chance to savor a glass of this delightful Polish beverage and experience the essence of Polish culture sip by sip.

Chapter 8.Homemade Beverages

Homemade beverages are an integral part of Polish cuisine and play a significant role in the country's culinary traditions. These beverages are not only refreshing but also hold cultural and historical value. They are often made from simple ingredients found in Polish households and showcase the resourcefulness and creativity of Polish people.

One of the most popular homemade beverages in Polish cuisine is kompot. Kompot is a traditional drink made by simmering a combination of fruits, such as apples, pears, plums, and berries, with water and sugar. It is usually served cold and is enjoyed during the summer season. Kompot is known for its refreshing taste and ability to quench thirst, making it a staple beverage in Polish households. The use of seasonal fruits adds variety to kompot, as different fruits are used depending on the time of year. This not only provides a delicious beverage but also allows Poles to utilize surplus fruits and prevent food waste.

Another homemade beverage that holds significance in Polish culture is miod pitny, or Polish mead. Mead is an ancient alcoholic beverage made by fermenting honey with water and yeast. It has a rich history in Poland and is often associated with special occasions and celebrations. Polish mead is known for its smooth and sweet taste, and it comes in various flavors and strengths. It is usually served slightly chilled and enjoyed in small glasses. Mead is often considered a symbol of Polish hospitality and is a common gift during weddings or other important events.

In addition to kompot and mead, homemade herb and fruit-infused vodkas are also popular in Polish cuisine. These vodkas, known as nalewki, are made by macerating fruits, berries, or herbs in alcohol. The resulting infusions are sweet, flavorful, and have a unique taste. Nalewki are often enjoyed as digestifs after meals or served as an aperitif before a meal. They are also frequently used in cocktail recipes, showcasing their versatility and importance in Polish beverage culture.

Homemade beverages in Polish cuisine not only provide a refreshing taste but also reflect the country's history and traditions. They demonstrate the resourcefulness of Polish people in utilizing local ingredients and preserving their cultural heritage. Whether it's the simplicity of kompot, the elegance of mead, or the variety of nalewki, these homemade beverages hold a special place in Polish households and are cherished by both locals and visitors alike.

9.1 Raising a Glass to Tradition

Polish cuisine is steeped in tradition, and it is evident in the importance placed on raising a glass to toast the rich culinary heritage of the country. This act not only pays homage to the past but also celebrates the present and highlights the significance of food and drink in Polish culture.

First and foremost, raising a glass to tradition in Polish cuisine is a way of honoring the historical roots of the country's culinary practices. Poland has a long and storied history, and its cuisine reflects the influences of neighboring countries, as well as its own cultural heritage. The act of raising a glass to tradition acknowledges the centuries-old recipes and techniques that have been passed down through generations, preserving the authentic flavors and techniques that make Polish cuisine unique.

Furthermore, raising a glass to tradition serves as a means of celebrating the present and the vibrant food scene that exists in Poland today. Traditional dishes are still widely enjoyed and cherished, both within the country and by those who appreciate Polish cuisine worldwide. From hearty pierogi filled with various ingredients to fragrant borscht soup and tender bigos, each dish tells a story of culinary excellence and showcases the skill of Polish chefs. Raising a glass to tradition is a testament to the ongoing appreciation and support for these dishes, ensuring that they remain an integral part of Polish cuisine for years to come.

In addition to honoring the past and celebrating the present, raising a glass to tradition also underscores the significance of food and drink in Polish culture. Sharing a meal and raising a glass together is a deeply rooted custom and a symbol of camaraderie. It signifies the importance of gathering with loved ones, friends, and even strangers to bond over a shared love of food. From festive occasions like weddings and holidays to everyday gatherings, the act of raising a glass is a way of fostering connections and strengthening relationships.

Raising a glass to tradition in the Polish cuisine is a meaningful and symbolic act. It pays tribute to the historical roots of the country's culinary practices, celebrates the present food scene, and highlights the role of food and drink in Polish culture. By embracing and appreciating the traditions of Polish cuisine, we not only preserve the rich heritage but also continue to create lasting memories and connections through the joy of food. So let us raise our glasses and toast to the timeless traditions of Polish cuisine. Na zdrowie!

9.1.1 Kawa z Mlekiem: Coffee with Milk

Kawa z Mlekiem, which translates to Coffee with Milk, is an essential part of Polish cuisine. This traditional Polish beverage holds great importance in the daily lives of the Polish people and has become deeply ingrained in their culture.

Poland has a long-standing history with coffee, dating back to the 17th century when it was introduced by the Ottoman Empire. Over time, the way coffee is consumed in Poland has evolved, and Kawa z Mlekiem has emerged as a popular choice. This coffee drink is typically made by combining a shot of espresso with steamed milk, resulting in a creamy and aromatic beverage.

One reason for the importance of Kawa z Mlekiem in Polish cuisine is its role in social gatherings. In Poland, coffee houses have historically been a meeting place for intellectuals, artists, and the general public. These coffee houses served as a hub for exchanging ideas and fostering discussions. Kawa z Mlekiem became a symbol of these gatherings, as people came together to enjoy a cup of coffee while engaging in meaningful conversations.

Furthermore, Kawa z Mlekiem is often associated with breakfast in Poland. It is a common practice for Poles to start their day with a cup of this coffee. The combination of coffee and milk provides a boost of energy, helping individuals kickstart their mornings. It is also accompanied by various traditional Polish breakfast foods such as scrambled eggs, sausages, and bread, making it a complete and satisfying meal.

Another reason for the importance of Kawa z Mlekiem is its comforting and nostalgic nature. For many Poles, this beverage triggers memories of their childhood or moments shared with loved ones. The familiar aroma and taste evoke a sense of warmth and security, providing a feeling of home. It is no wonder that Kawa z Mlekiem is often served during family gatherings or special occasions, creating a sense of tradition and nostalgia.

In addition to its cultural significance, Kawa z Mlekiem is also regarded for its taste and quality. Polish baristas take pride in preparing this coffee drink meticulously, ensuring the perfect balance between espresso and milk. The skill and expertise required to create a harmonious blend of flavors are deeply respected and appreciated in Poland.

Kawa z Mlekiem holds immense importance in the Polish cuisine. Its role as a social drink, breakfast staple, and source of comfort make it an integral part of Polish culture. Whether enjoyed in a bustling coffee house or within the cozy confines of home, Kawa z Mlekiem embodies the essence of Polish hospitality and tradition.

9.1.2 Kisiel (Fruit Jelly Drink)

Kisiel, a popular fruit jelly drink, holds great importance in Polish cuisine. This traditional Polish dessert has been enjoyed for centuries and continues to be a beloved treat for all ages.

One of the main reasons why Kisiel is highly valued in Polish cuisine is its refreshing and light nature. Made from fruit juice, water, and sugar, Kisiel has a smooth and silky texture that provides a delightful experience for the palate. Its natural fruity flavors add a burst of sweetness without overshadowing the other flavors in a meal.

Kisiel is not only appreciated for its taste but also for its versatility. It can be enjoyed on its own as a tasty treat or used as a topping for various desserts such as ice cream, cakes, and pancakes. Its vibrant colors and luscious consistency make it visually appealing, often enhancing the overall presentation of a dish.

Furthermore, Kisiel holds cultural significance in Poland. It is commonly served during family gatherings, celebrations, and holidays. It has become a symbol of Polish hospitality and plays a role in preserving culinary traditions. The preparation and consumption of Kisiel has been passed down through generations, creating a sense of nostalgia and unity among Polish households.

From a nutritional standpoint, Kisiel offers a healthier alternative to many sugary drinks. It is often made from fresh fruits, providing essential vitamins and minerals. Its lower sugar content makes it a favorable option for those who are conscious of their health.

Kisiel plays a significant role in Polish cuisine due to its delightful taste, versatility, cultural importance, and nutritional value. It is both a cherished dessert and a symbol of Polish heritage. Whether enjoyed on its own or used as a complement to other dishes, Kisiel continues to be an integral part of the Polish dining experience.

Chapter 9. Traditional Celebrations and Holidays

Traditional Celebrations and Holidays play a significant role in Polish Cuisine. These festivities are deeply rooted in Polish culture and are celebrated with great enthusiasm and joy. They showcase the rich culinary traditions and customs passed down through generations.

One of the most significant traditional celebrations is Wigilia, which takes place on Christmas Eve. It is a time of fasting and reflection for Catholics and involves a meticulously prepared meatless feast known as "the twelve dishes." Traditional dishes include beetroot soup (borscht), dumplings filled with cabbage and mushrooms (pierogi), carp in aspic, and poppy seed cake (makowiec). These dishes symbolize various aspects of the Catholic faith and are meant to bring good fortune and unity to the family.

Easter is another important holiday in Poland, and it is associated with numerous culinary traditions. One of the signature dishes is żurek, a sour rye soup traditionally served with white sausage and hard-boiled eggs. Another popular dish is pascha, a sweet cheese dessert adorned with dried fruits, almonds, and chocolate. Additionally, the Easter table is decorated with a wide variety of regional dishes, such as roasted lamb, beetroot salad, and homemade babka (a festive yeast cake).

May 3rd, known as Constitution Day, is an occasion to celebrate Polish heritage and independence. On this day, families often gather for a picnic or barbecue. Grilled sausages (kiełbasa) and zrazy (stuffed beef rolls) are commonly enjoyed, along with traditional salads like mizeria (cucumber and sour cream salad) and sałatka jarzynowa (vegetable salad). These dishes reflect the joyful atmosphere of the holiday and the appreciation for freedom.

Traditional celebrations and holidays showcase the importance of family and togetherness in Polish culture. They provide a platform for passing down culinary traditions from one generation to the next, ensuring the preservation of cultural heritage. These celebrations not only bring people together but also serve as an opportunity to reconnect with Polish identity and history.

Traditional celebrations and holidays greatly contribute to the richness of Polish Cuisine. They not only provide a glimpse into the country's cultural heritage but also offer a chance for individuals to experience and appreciate the flavors, customs, and values that have shaped Polish cuisine over the centuries.

10.1 A Taste of Polish Holidays

Polish holidays are filled with rich traditions and delicious food. One of the highlights of these celebrations is the diverse and flavorful cuisine that is enjoyed during special occasions. We will explore the importance of the traditional Polish holiday dishes and their significance in Polish culture.

Firstly, Polish holidays such as Christmas, Easter, and New Year's Eve are all celebrated with great enthusiasm and the culinary traditions associated with these occasions are deeply rooted in Polish heritage. These festive meals not only satisfy the hunger but also bring families and friends together, creating an atmosphere of warmth and togetherness.

One iconic Polish holiday dish is "Barszcz" which is a traditional beet soup usually served during Christmas Eve dinner. It is known for its vibrant red color and its tangy-sweet flavor. Barszcz represents the abundance and prosperity of the upcoming year and is believed to bring good luck to those who consume it.

Another popular dish is "Pierogi", which are filled dumplings that come in various flavors such as potato and cheese, sauerkraut and mushroom, or fruit-filled for dessert. Pierogi are commonly served during Christmas and Easter, symbolizing unity and family bonding. The process of making pierogi is often a group effort, with family members coming together to roll out the dough, shape the dumplings, and fill them with love and care.

"Kutia" is a traditional Christmas dessert made from wheat grains, honey, and various nuts. It is typically enjoyed after the Christmas Eve dinner and represents the importance of harvest and gratitude for the abundance of food. Kutia is a symbolic dish that connects generations and is often prepared using age-old family recipes that are passed down through the years.

Furthermore, "Bigos" is a hearty hunter's stew that is often prepared for New Year's Eve. This dish combines various meats, including sausage, pork, and beef, with sauerkraut, mushrooms, and spices. Bigos is slowly cooked for hours, allowing the flavors to blend together and create a delicious and comforting meal. It symbolizes the coming together of different ingredients and traditions, just like the diverse Polish culture itself.

Polish holidays are not only about celebrating traditions and spending time with loved ones but also about enjoying the delectable dishes that are an integral part of these celebrations. The taste of Polish holidays is deeply rooted in the values of togetherness, unity, and gratitude. From the vibrant barszcz to the comforting pierogi and the symbolic kutia, these traditional dishes play a significant role in connecting generations and preserving Polish cultural heritage. So, the next time you experience a taste of Polish holidays, remember the centuries-old traditions and the heartfelt meaning behind each dish.

10.1.1 Wigilia: Polish Christmas Eve

Wigilia, the Polish Christmas Eve, holds immense importance in Polish cuisine. It is considered the most significant holiday of the year, where families gather around the table to share a festive meal and celebrate the birth of Jesus Christ.

One of the unique aspects of Wigilia is the tradition of the "12 dishes." According to the Polish custom, twelve meatless dishes are served, symbolizing the twelve apostles. Each dish is meticulously prepared and holds a special meaning. Some traditional Wigilia dishes include barszcz (beetroot soup), uszka (mushroom-filled dumplings), pierogi (stuffed dumplings), and kutia (sweet grain pudding). These dishes are not only delicious but also deeply rooted in Polish culture and tradition.

The Wigilia meal is rich in symbolism and reflects the spirit of Christmas. The dishes are carefully chosen to represent different virtues such as hope, prosperity, and joy. For instance, barszcz (beetroot soup) symbolizes goodwill, while kutia symbolizes humility and gratitude for the harvest. Each dish tells a story and carries a message of love, unity, and faith.

Wigilia is not just about the food; it is a time for families to come together and share meaningful moments. The preparation of the meal often involves the whole family, with each member contributing their skills and traditions. It is a time for bonding, reminiscing, and passing down family recipes from generation to generation.

Moreover, Wigilia is deeply connected to Polish traditions and customs. The meal is typically served after the first star appears in the sky, representing the Star of Bethlehem. Before the meal, the family gathers to share the opłatek, a thin wafer, and exchange wishes for the upcoming year. The atmosphere during Wigilia is filled with warmth, love, and a sense of togetherness.

Wigilia also showcases the richness and diversity of Polish cuisine. Each region of Poland has its own unique dishes and culinary traditions, adding to the vibrant tapestry of Polish Christmas Eve. These regional variations make Wigilia a dynamic and exciting celebration of Polish heritage.

Wigilia: Polish Christmas Eve holds great importance in Polish cuisine. It not only showcases the culinary riches of Poland but also embodies the spirit of Christmas, family, and traditions. The tradition of the "12 dishes," the symbolism behind each meal, and the significance of family bonding make Wigilia a truly special occasion. It is a time to cherish, appreciate, and celebrate the cultural legacy of the Polish people.

10.1.2 Easter Feasts

Easter Feasts hold great importance in Polish Cuisine. The tradition of Easter Feasts in Poland dates back centuries and is deeply rooted in religious and cultural practices.

Polish Easter Feasts are characterized by a variety of traditional dishes and customs that are observed during this festive season. One of the most significant dishes is the "Święconka," which is a blessed food basket containing various symbolic elements. The basket typically includes bread, eggs, salt, horseradish, ham, and lamb-shaped butter. Each of these items holds a special meaning and represents different aspects of the Easter story.

The main course of the Easter Feast often consists of a roasted or smoked ham, accompanied by a variety of side dishes. Popular side dishes include "Żurek," a sour rye soup with sausage and boiled eggs, and "Babka," a sweet yeast cake with raisins. Other traditional foods that are commonly served include "Pierogi" (dumplings) filled with cheese, potatoes, sauerkraut, or fruit, and "Kiełbasa" (Polish sausage).

Easter Feasts are also known for the abundance of desserts and sweets. One well-loved dessert is the "Mazurek," a flat cake topped with various types of fruit, nuts, or chocolate. Additionally, "Sernik" (Polish cheesecake) and "Piernik" (gingerbread) are popular treats during this time.

Apart from the culinary aspect, Easter Feasts in Poland also involve cultural and religious traditions. Families gather together to share a festive meal, exchange wishes, and participate in Easter egg decorating. The art of decorating Easter eggs, known as "Pisanki," is a cherished tradition, with intricate designs and vibrant colors.

The significance of Easter Feasts in Polish Cuisine goes beyond the enjoyment of food. It is a time for families to come together, celebrate their faith, and honor their cultural heritage. These feasts not only nourish the body but also the spirit, creating lasting memories and strengthening bonds between loved ones.

Chapter 10.   Tips and Techniques

Polish Cuisine holds a rich history and diverse range of flavors that have been shaped by various factors, including geography, cultural influences, and historical developments. We will explore some tips and techniques that are integral to the Polish culinary tradition.

1. Traditional Ingredients:

Polish cuisine is known for its use of hearty ingredients such as meat, potatoes, cabbage, beets, and mushrooms. These ingredients are often locally sourced and reflect the country's agricultural heritage.

2. Polish Flavors:

The Polish culinary palette is characterized by a balance of savory and hearty flavors. Dishes often incorporate herbs and spices like dill, marjoram, caraway seeds, and black pepper. Traditional Polish cuisine also includes a variety of pickled ingredients, adding tanginess and complexity to the flavors.

3. Pierogi - The Iconic Dish:

Pierogi, delicious filled dumplings, are an integral part of Polish cuisine. The dough is typically made using flour, water, and sometimes eggs, resulting in a soft and tender texture. Fillings range from savory options like potato and cheese, sauerkraut and mushroom, or meat, to sweet fillings like fruit or sweet cheese.

4. Polish Soups:

Soup holds an important place in Polish cuisine. Zurek, Barszcz, and Rosół are some of the popular traditional soups. Zurek, a sour rye soup, is made from fermented rye flour and often includes ingredients like sausages, boiled eggs, and root vegetables. Barszcz, a beetroot soup, is known for its vibrant color and can be enjoyed hot or cold. Rosół is a simple chicken broth often served with homemade noodles or dumplings.

5. Slow Cooking and Braising:

Many authentic Polish dishes require slow cooking or braising techniques to develop rich flavors. Popular examples include bigos, a hunter's stew made with sauerkraut, fresh cabbage, and various cuts of meat, and gołąbki, cabbage rolls filled with a mixture of ground meat, rice, and spices, simmered in tomato sauce.

6. Bread and Pastries:

Bread, particularly rye bread, is a staple in Polish cuisine. Traditional Polish bakeries offer a wide variety of bread and pastries, including Babka, Makowiec (poppy seed roll), and Piernik (gingerbread).

7. Festive Foods:

Polish cuisine also boasts a range of dishes specifically prepared for festive occasions. For example, during Christmas, Poles often enjoy dishes like barszcz with uszka (beet soup with mushroom-filled dumplings), carp, pierogi with various fillings, and kutia (a sweet grain and nut dessert).

These tips and techniques provide a glimpse into the rich culinary heritage of Polish cuisine. From the comforting flavors of hearty soups to the delicate dough of pierogi, Polish cuisine continues to delight food enthusiasts around the world with its unique and diverse offerings.

11.1 Mastering Dumpling-Making

Polish cuisine is known for its delicious and hearty dishes, and one of the most beloved culinary treasures is dumplings. Dumplings are a traditional Polish dish that comes in various fillings and shapes, making them versatile and satisfying. Mastering the art of dumpling-making in Polish cuisine can be a rewarding experience, allowing you to indulge in homemade delicacies that will impress your family and friends.

To begin your journey to becoming a master dumpling-maker, you first need to familiarize yourself with the different types of dumplings in Polish cuisine. Pierogi is the most well-known and widely consumed type of dumpling in Poland. They are typically semicircular or crescent-shaped and filled with a variety of ingredients such as potatoes, cheese, sauerkraut, mushrooms, or meat. Another popular type of Polish dumpling is Uszka, which are small, twisted dumplings often served in clear broth during Christmas Eve supper.

The key to mastering the art of dumpling-making lies in the dough. Traditional Polish dumpling dough is made from flour, water, and a pinch of salt. The dough is rolled out into thin sheets and then cut into circles or squares, depending on the shape of the dumplings you wish to make. The filling is placed in the center of each dumpling, and then the edges are carefully sealed together to create a pocket of deliciousness.

When it comes to fillings, the possibilities are endless. For potato and cheese pierogi, mashed potatoes are mixed with farmer's cheese, onions, salt, and pepper. For mushroom pierogi, sautéed mushrooms are combined with onions and seasoned to perfection. Meat-filled pierogi often consist of ground pork or beef mixed with onions, garlic, and various spices. Sauerkraut and cabbage are also popular fillings, adding a tangy and savory element to the dumplings.

To cook the dumplings, bring a large pot of salted water to a boil. Gently drop the dumplings into the boiling water and cook until they float to the surface, which usually takes about 3-4 minutes. Be careful not to overcrowd the pot, as the dumplings need space to cook evenly.

Once cooked, Polish dumplings can be enjoyed in various ways. Some like to serve them with melted butter, crispy bacon bits, and caramelized onions, while others prefer sour cream or a dollop of plain yogurt. Regardless of how you choose to garnish them, the flavors and textures of the dumplings will leave you craving more.

Practice is key to mastering dumpling-making in Polish cuisine. Start with simple fillings and shapes, gradually experimenting with more complex combinations and techniques. Don't be discouraged if your first attempts are not perfect - remember that practice makes perfect, and the reward of enjoying your homemade dumplings will be well worth the effort.

Mastering the art of dumpling-making in Polish cuisine opens up a world of flavors and culinary delights. From the comforting potato and cheese pierogi to the elegant Uszka served in broth, Polish dumplings are a true treat for the senses. With a bit of practice and a love for cooking, you can become a master dumpling-maker and impress your loved ones with your homemade Polish delicacies.

11.1.1 Rolling, Filling, and Shaping Dumplings

Dumplings, known as pierogi, are a beloved dish in Polish cuisine. They are versatile, delicious, and can be enjoyed as a main course or a side dish. Making pierogi from scratch involves three main steps:

rolling the dough, filling it, and shaping the dumplings. We will delve into each of these steps and explore the techniques used in Polish cuisine.

The first step in making pierogi is rolling the dough. Traditionally, the dough is made by mixing flour, water, and sometimes eggs until it forms a smooth and elastic consistency. This dough is then rolled out using a rolling pin on a lightly floured surface. The aim is to achieve a thin and uniform thickness, which will ensure that the dumplings cook evenly.

Once the dough is rolled out, it is time to move on to the filling. Polish cuisine offers a wide variety of fillings for pierogi, ranging from savory to sweet. Some popular savory fillings include mashed potatoes with cheese, sauerkraut with mushrooms, and meat fillings such as ground pork or beef. Sweet fillings often feature fruits like blueberries or cherries, accompanied by a touch of sugar. Regardless of the filling, it is important to ensure that it is well-seasoned and evenly distributed on the dough.

Shaping the dumplings is an art in itself. Traditional Polish pierogi are typically shaped into half-moons or triangles. To shape a half-moon, a small portion of filling is placed in the center of a circular piece of dough. The edges of the dough are then folded over to seal the filling, creating a crescent shape. To make triangular-shaped pierogi, the circular piece of dough is folded in half, forming a semicircle. The edges are then sealed, creating the desired triangular shape.

It is worth noting that there are countless regional and family variations when it comes to shaping pierogi. Some particularly skilled cooks can even create intricate patterns using small pleats or twists. These unique shapes not only add visual appeal but also help to hold the filling securely, ensuring that no deliciousness is lost during the cooking process.

Rolling, filling, and shaping dumplings is a labor of love in Polish cuisine. Each step requires skill and attention to detail to achieve the perfect pierogi. From the thin and elastic dough to the flavorful fillings and artfully shaped dumplings, Polish pierogi are a true delight to both make and savor. So why not gather some friends or family members, roll up your sleeves, and embark on a pierogi-making adventure? Your taste buds will be eternally grateful.

11.1.2 Boiling, Frying, or Baking Dumplings

Boiling, frying, and baking are all common cooking methods used in the Polish cuisine to prepare dumplings. Each method has its own distinct characteristics, resulting in different textures and flavors.

Boiling dumplings is a traditional method used to cook Polish dumplings, known as pierogi. To boil dumplings, start by bringing a pot of water to a boil. Add the dumplings to the boiling water and cook them until they float to the surface, which usually takes around 2-3 minutes. Boiled dumplings have a tender and soft texture, with a slightly chewy and doughy exterior. This cooking method is often preferred for potato or cheese-filled dumplings.

Frying dumplings, also known as pan-frying or sautéing, is another popular way of preparing dumplings in Polish cuisine. To fry dumplings, heat a pan over medium heat and add a small amount of oil or butter. Place the dumplings in the pan and cook them for a few minutes on each side until they turn golden brown and crispy. Frying dumplings gives them a crispy exterior while maintaining a tender and juicy filling. This method is commonly used for meat-filled dumplings, such as those filled with ground pork or beef.

Baking dumplings is a less common but equally delicious method used in Polish cuisine. To bake dumplings, preheat the oven to a moderate temperature. Place the dumplings on a baking sheet or in a baking dish and bake them for around 20-25 minutes or until they are cooked through and the exterior is golden brown. Baking dumplings results in a slightly firmer texture compared to boiling or frying, with a crispy exterior and a soft interior. This method is typically used for fruit-filled dumplings like cherry or apple.

Whichever cooking method you choose, boiling, frying, or baking dumplings in the Polish cuisine allows you to enjoy the delicious flavors and textures of this traditional dish. Experiment with different fillings and cooking techniques to discover your favorite way to prepare and enjoy Polish dumplings.

Chapter 11. Kitchen Staples and Essential Recipes

Polish cuisine is known for its rich flavors and hearty dishes. This will explore the kitchen staples and essential recipes that are integral to Polish cooking.

One of the key kitchen staples in Polish cuisine is potatoes. Potatoes are a versatile ingredient and are used in many traditional Polish dishes. They are often boiled or mashed and served as a side dish, but they can also be used as a main ingredient in dishes like potato pancakes or potato dumplings.

Another important ingredient in Polish cuisine is cabbage. Cabbage is used in a variety of dishes, including sauerkraut, which is fermented cabbage. Sauerkraut is often served as a side dish or used as a filling for pierogi, which are dumplings filled with various fillings.

Meat is also a staple in Polish cuisine. Popular meat dishes include bigos, which is a hunter's stew made with a combination of various meats, sausages, and sauerkraut. Another favorite is golabki, which are cabbage rolls filled with a mixture of meat, rice, and spices.

One of the essential recipes in Polish cuisine is pierogi. Pierogi are dumplings filled with various fillings, such as potatoes and cheese, sauerkraut and mushrooms, or meat. They are typically boiled and then pan-fried until golden brown. Pierogi are often served with sour cream or melted butter.

Another essential recipe is borscht, which is a beet soup. Borscht is made by simmering beets, vegetables, and sometimes meat in a broth. It is often served hot with a dollop of sour cream on top.

Lastly, Polish cuisine is known for its sweet treats. One of the most popular desserts is paczki, which are deep-fried doughnuts filled with various sweet fillings, such as jam or custard. Another favorite is szarlotka, which is a Polish apple pie made with a buttery, crumbly crust and a sweet apple filling.

Polish cuisine has a variety of kitchen staples and essential recipes that are integral to its rich and flavorful dishes. From potatoes and cabbage to pierogi and borscht, Polish cooking offers a wide range of delicious options for food enthusiasts to explore.

12.1 Crafting Homemade Pierogi Dough

Crafting homemade Pierogi dough is an essential practice in Polish cuisine. These delightful dumplings are a significant part of the country's culinary heritage and have become popular worldwide. The process of making homemade Pierogi dough involves a few basic ingredients, including flour, water, eggs, and salt, which are skillfully combined to create a chewy, yet tender dough that perfectly complements the flavorful fillings found inside.

One of the main advantages of crafting homemade Pierogi dough is the ability to control the quality of ingredients used. By preparing the dough from scratch, one can ensure that only fresh, high-quality ingredients are used, resulting in a superior final product. This attention to detail sets homemade Pierogi apart from those made with store-bought dough, which may contain preservatives or additives.

The act of making Pierogi dough by hand also carries cultural significance. In Polish households, the process of preparing homemade Pierogi is often a communal activity involving family or friends. This tradition fosters a sense of togetherness and bond-building, as generations pass down techniques and family recipes. The act of rolling out the dough, filling it, and sealing it together creates a shared experience that connects individuals to their heritage and culinary roots.

Another reason why crafting homemade Pierogi dough is important is the versatility it offers. While the classic Pierogi filling is made with potatoes and cheese, the dough can accommodate various fillings ranging from savory to sweet. Popular alternatives include sauerkraut and mushroom, meat, fruit, and even chocolate. This adaptability allows for endless creativity in exploring different flavor combinations and satisfying individual preferences, making homemade Pierogi a versatile dish that can be enjoyed in numerous contexts.

Furthermore, making homemade Pierogi dough allows for customization and adaptation according to dietary requirements or restrictions. By substituting ingredients or altering proportions, individuals can create gluten-free, vegan, or other specialized versions of the dough to accommodate personal dietary preferences. This inclusivity ensures that everyone can partake in the joy of enjoying Pierogi without compromising their dietary needs.

Crafting homemade Pierogi dough holds immense importance in Polish cuisine. By preparing the dough from scratch, individuals can control the quality of ingredients, preserve cultural traditions, and explore a wide range of filling options. The act of making Pierogi dough by hand promotes togetherness and creates a sense of connection to one's heritage. Additionally, customization options cater to diverse dietary needs, allowing everyone to experience the delights of Pierogi. Whether eaten as a main dish, appetizer, or dessert, homemade Pierogi is a culinary masterpiece that captures the essence of Polish cuisine.

12.1.1 Preparing Traditional Polish Sauerkraut

Preparing traditional Polish sauerkraut is an essential aspect of Polish cuisine. Sauerkraut, also known as "kapusta kiszona" in Polish, holds great significance in the country's culinary heritage and continues to be a popular ingredient in many traditional dishes.

To prepare traditional Polish sauerkraut, the process typically starts with finding the right type of cabbage. The most suitable cabbage variety for sauerkraut is the white cabbage, as it has a firm texture and high water content, making it ideal for fermentation. The cabbage is shredded into thin strips or finely chopped, and then salt is added to draw out the moisture.

The next step in preparing sauerkraut is fermentation. The cabbage is packed tightly into a clean jar or fermenting crock, ensuring that there are no air pockets. The cabbage needs to be fully submerged in its own liquid to promote fermentation and prevent the growth of harmful bacteria. It is important to weight down the cabbage to keep it submerged, as exposure to air can result in spoilage.

During fermentation, the natural bacteria present on the cabbage convert the sugars into lactic acid, giving sauerkraut its distinct sour taste and providing numerous health benefits. This lactic acid fermentation process also helps preserve the sauerkraut for an extended period.

Traditional Polish sauerkraut is often flavored with various ingredients to enhance its taste. Caraway seeds, juniper berries, apples, and garlic are commonly added to the sauerkraut during the fermentation process. These additional flavors contribute to the complexity of the sauerkraut, resulting in a well-rounded and delicious condiment.

The importance of preparing traditional Polish sauerkraut in Polish cuisine lies in its versatility and contribution to the overall flavor profile of many dishes. Sauerkraut is a key component in many traditional Polish recipes, such as "bigos" (hunter's stew), "pierogi" (dumplings), and "kotlet schabowy" (breaded pork cutlet). It adds a tangy and slightly acidic taste, balancing out the richness of meat-based dishes and providing a unique culinary experience.

Furthermore, sauerkraut is known for its numerous health benefits. It is rich in probiotics, which support a healthy gut microbiome and aid in digestion. Sauerkraut also contains high levels of vitamin C and other essential nutrients, making it a nutritious addition to meals.

In summary, preparing traditional Polish sauerkraut holds great importance in Polish cuisine. Its unique fermentation process, added flavors, and versatility make it a cherished ingredient in many traditional dishes. The distinct sour taste and health benefits of sauerkraut contribute to its widespread popularity and make it an integral part of Polish culinary heritage.

12.1.2 Creating Your Borscht Base

Creating Your Borscht Base is essential in Polish cuisine as it forms the foundation for a flavorful and traditional dish. Borscht, a beet soup, is widely enjoyed in Poland and is known for its vibrant color and rich taste. The base of borscht consists of ingredients such as beets, onions, carrots, garlic, and celery, which are sautéed in butter or oil until they become tender and aromatic.

The importance of creating a proper borscht base lies in the depth of flavor it adds to the soup. The combination of sautéed vegetables creates a savory and slightly sweet undertone that complements the earthiness of the beets. This base acts as a flavor enhancer and sets the stage for a delicious bowl of borscht.

Another key aspect of the borscht base is the cooking technique. Slowly simmering the base allows the flavors to meld together and develop a robust taste. This slow and patient cooking process is essential to fully extract the essence of the vegetables and create a harmonious blend of flavors.

Furthermore, the color of borscht is a defining characteristic, and the base plays a crucial role in achieving that vibrant deep red hue. The beets used in the base provide natural pigments that infuse the soup with its striking color. The longer the base is simmered, the more vibrant and intense the color becomes, making for an aesthetically pleasing dish.

Creating Your Borscht Base is not only important for the taste and appearance of the soup but also for preserving Polish culinary traditions. Borscht has been a staple in Polish cuisine for centuries, and the base is a fundamental part of the recipe that has been passed down through generations. By honoring the tradition of making the borscht base, we keep the authentic flavors alive and ensure that the essence of Polish cuisine is preserved.

Creating Your Borscht Base is of utmost importance in Polish cuisine. It adds depth of flavor, enhances the color, and maintains the authenticity of this beloved dish. Taking the time and care to create a flavorful base sets the stage for a delicious and satisfying bowl of borscht that pays homage to Polish culinary traditions.

Chapter 12. Healthy Twists on Polish Classics

Polish cuisine is known for its hearty and flavorful dishes that are loved by many. However, with the rise in health consciousness, there is a growing demand for healthier options that still preserve the essence of traditional Polish cooking. This is where the concept of healthy twists on Polish classics comes into play.

Introducing healthy twists on Polish classics allows individuals to enjoy their favorite dishes while also taking care of their health. By making simple substitutions and modifications, traditional Polish recipes can be transformed into nutritious and balanced meals.

One example of a healthy twist is the use of whole grain or gluten-free flours in place of refined white flour. This not only adds a nutty flavor to dishes like pierogi or naleśniki but also increases the dietary fiber content, making them more satiating and beneficial for digestion.

Another healthy tweak is reducing the amount of salt and fat used in traditional recipes. Polish cuisine often uses a generous amount of butter, cream, and salt, which can contribute to health issues like high blood pressure and cholesterol. By using healthier alternatives such as olive oil, lean meats, and low-fat dairy products, the nutritional profile of dishes improves without compromising on taste.

Additionally, incorporating more vegetables and lean proteins into traditional Polish dishes is another way to promote healthiness. Adding colorful vegetables like spinach, kale, and bell peppers not only enhances the visual appeal of the dish but also increases the vitamin and mineral content. Lean proteins such as chicken, turkey, or tofu can replace heavier meats like pork or beef, reducing the calorie and fat content while still providing essential nutrients.

Furthermore, utilizing traditional Polish herbs and spices such as dill, parsley, and paprika can provide additional flavors without relying on excessive salt or unhealthy seasonings. These herbs and spices not only add depth to the dish but also offer various health benefits, such as anti-inflammatory properties and antioxidants.

Overall, the importance of healthy twists on Polish classics lies in creating a balance between tradition and modern dietary preferences. By incorporating healthier ingredients and cooking techniques, Polish cuisine can continue to evolve and cater to a wider range of individuals. These twists not only enhance the nutritional content of dishes but also encourage people to explore the diverse flavors and possibilities within Polish cuisine.

13.1 Lighter Versions of Traditional Favorites

The Polish cuisine is known for its hearty and flavorful dishes, often prepared using traditional recipes that have been passed down through generations. However, with increasing health concerns and a growing emphasis on maintaining a balanced diet, there is a need for lighter versions of these traditional favorites.

One of the main reasons why lighter versions of traditional Polish dishes are important is because they provide a healthier alternative without compromising on taste. Traditional dishes such as pierogi (filled dumplings), kielbasa (sausage), and bigos (hunter's stew) are often high in fat and calories. By creating lighter versions of these dishes, individuals can enjoy the flavors they love while also making healthier choices.

Incorporating lighter ingredients and cooking techniques can help reduce the calorie and fat content of traditional Polish dishes. For example, instead of using regular pasta dough for pierogi, whole wheat or spinach dough can be used to add more fiber and nutrients. Leaner cuts of meat can be used in kielbasa, and vegetables can be added to increase the nutritional value of bigos.

Lighter versions of traditional favorites also make Polish cuisine more inclusive and accessible to individuals with dietary restrictions or preferences. Many people today follow specific diets, such as vegetarian, vegan, or gluten-free, for various reasons. By adapting traditional recipes to meet these dietary needs, a wider audience can enjoy the taste and cultural experience of Polish cuisine.

Furthermore, lighter versions of traditional Polish dishes can help promote sustainability and reduce the environmental impact of food production. For example, using more plant-based ingredients in place of meat can help decrease the carbon footprint associated with livestock farming. Additionally, by encouraging the use of local and seasonal produce, lighter Polish dishes can support local farmers and reduce the transportation emissions associated with importing ingredients.

The importance of lighter versions of traditional favorites in Polish cuisine cannot be overstated. They offer a healthier alternative without compromising on taste, cater to individuals with dietary restrictions, promote sustainability, and can help make Polish cuisine more inclusive. By embracing lighter variations of traditional dishes, we can ensure that the rich culinary heritage of Poland continues to evolve and adapt to meet the needs and preferences of a changing world.

13.1.1 Vegan Cabbage Rolls

Vegan Cabbage Rolls have gained significant importance in Polish cuisine. These delicious dishes are typically made by wrapping cabbage leaves around a filling of grains, legumes, and vegetables. While traditional cabbage rolls are usually prepared with meat, the rise of veganism has led to the creation of plant-based alternatives.

The importance of Vegan Cabbage Rolls lies in their cultural significance and health benefits. In Polish culture, cabbage has been a staple ingredient for centuries, and the development of vegan variations expands the culinary options for those who prefer plant-based diets. Vegan Cabbage Rolls also cater to individuals with dietary restrictions, such as vegetarians and vegans, and promote inclusivity within the Polish culinary tradition.

From a health perspective, Vegan Cabbage Rolls offer numerous benefits. Cabbage is a nutritious vegetable high in fiber, vitamins C and K, and antioxidants. The filling ingredients, including grains and legumes, provide essential nutrients like protein, iron, and B vitamins. These plant-based ingredients contribute to a well-balanced diet and support overall health and well-being.

Vegan Cabbage Rolls also contribute to environmental sustainability. Livestock production for meat consumption is a leading cause of greenhouse gas emissions, deforestation, and water pollution. By choosing vegan alternatives like Cabbage Rolls, individuals can reduce their carbon footprint and make a positive impact on the environment.

Vegan Cabbage Rolls have become an important and popular component in Polish cuisine. They provide a plant-based alternative to traditional meat-filled cabbage rolls, catering to dietary preferences and encouraging healthier, more sustainable food choices. With their cultural significance, health benefits, and positive impact on the environment, Vegan Cabbage Rolls have rightfully acquired a prominent place in Polish culinary traditions.

13.1.2 Gluten-Free Pierogi Options

The importance of gluten-free pierogi options in the Polish cuisine cannot be overstated. In recent years, there has been an increasing awareness and demand for gluten-free food options due to the rise in gluten sensitivities and celiac disease. This has prompted a need for traditional dishes to be adapted to cater to a wider range of dietary needs.

Pierogi, a popular Polish dish, typically consists of a dumpling filled with various ingredients such as cheese, potatoes, meat, or fruits. Traditionally, the dough for pierogi contains wheat flour, making it off-limits for individuals with gluten intolerance. However, with the introduction of gluten-free pierogi options, individuals with dietary restrictions can now enjoy this beloved dish without any worries.

One of the main reasons for the importance of gluten-free pierogi options in Polish cuisine is inclusivity. Poland has a rich culinary heritage, and pierogi has always been a symbol of Polish culture and tradition. By offering gluten-free alternatives, Polish cuisine becomes more accessible and welcoming to those with dietary restrictions. It allows individuals who may have previously been excluded from enjoying this iconic dish to partake in the cultural experience.

Furthermore, gluten-free pierogi options contribute to the overall health and well-being of individuals. Celiac disease affects an estimated 1% of the population, and consuming gluten can lead to severe health consequences for those with the condition. By offering gluten-free versions of pierogi, individuals with celiac disease can still enjoy this traditional dish without compromising their health.

In recent years, there has also been a growing interest in healthier eating habits and conscious food choices. Many individuals are adopting gluten-free diets for various reasons, including weight management and overall well-being. The availability of gluten-free pierogi options in Polish cuisine caters to this trend, allowing individuals to indulge in a beloved dish while adhering to their dietary preferences.

Lastly, the importance of gluten-free pierogi options lies in preserving culinary traditions for future generations. Traditional recipes hold a significant cultural and historical value, and it is vital to keep them alive. By adapting pierogi recipes to be gluten-free, the culinary heritage of Poland can be passed down to the next generation, ensuring that these traditional dishes continue to be enjoyed for years to come.

The importance of gluten-free pierogi options in the Polish cuisine is multifaceted. It promotes inclusivity, caters to the dietary needs of individuals with gluten sensitivities, contributes to overall health and well-being, and preserves culinary traditions. By offering gluten-free alternatives, Polish cuisine becomes more accessible, diverse, and adaptable to the changing dietary landscape. Thus, gluten-free pierogi options play a vital role in ensuring that everyone can enjoy the flavors and cultural significance of this beloved dish.

Chapter 13. Polish Fusion and Modern Cuisine

Polish Fusion and Modern Cuisine play a significant role in the evolution of Polish Cuisine. The combination of traditional Polish recipes with global culinary influences has resulted in a gastronomic revolution that is reshaping the country's culinary landscape.

Poland's historical and cultural background has greatly influenced its cuisine. Traditional Polish cuisine is known for its hearty and comforting dishes, such as pierogi, bigos, and kielbasa. However, in recent years, there has been a growing movement towards embracing new flavors, techniques, and ingredients from around the world.

Polish Fusion cuisine seeks to blend Polish traditions with international influences. Chefs are experimenting with incorporating ingredients and cooking methods from different cultures into classic Polish dishes. For example, you might find pierogi filled with Mexican-inspired ingredients like jalapenos and cheese or served with Asian-style dipping sauces.

This fusion of flavors not only showcases the creativity of Polish chefs but also introduces a new dining experience for both locals and tourists. The combination of familiar and foreign ingredients creates a unique culinary adventure, enticing diners to try new flavors and expand their palates.

Modern Cuisine in Poland goes beyond fusion and takes inspiration from global culinary trends. It incorporates innovative cooking techniques, artistic plating, and molecular gastronomy principles to create visually stunning and thought-provoking dishes. Chefs are pushing boundaries and reimagining traditional Polish ingredients in unexpected ways.

By embracing Polish Fusion and Modern Cuisine, Poland is not only attracting food enthusiasts from around the world but also breathing new life into its culinary heritage. These culinary movements have become a source of national pride as they highlight Poland's cultural diversity and culinary creativity.

Moreover, Polish Fusion and Modern Cuisine have paved the way for a new generation of Polish chefs to showcase their talent on the international culinary stage. Their innovative approaches and unique interpretations of traditional dishes have garnered recognition and acclaim globally.

Polish Fusion and Modern Cuisine have played a pivotal role in redefining Polish cuisine. They have brought exciting new flavors, techniques, and culinary perspectives to traditional dishes, creating a dynamic and diverse food scene. By embracing these culinary movements, Poland has made its mark on the global gastronomy map and continues to captivate food lovers with its rich and evolving food culture.

14.1 Modern Polish Flair

Polish cuisine is known for its rich and hearty flavors, and in recent years, a new trend has emerged - the incorporation of modern influences and techniques, creating what is now referred to as Modern Polish Flair. This new take on traditional Polish dishes has brought a fresh perspective to the country's culinary scene and has gained significant attention both locally and internationally.

One of the key aspects of Modern Polish Flair is the innovative use of ingredients. While traditional Polish cuisine heavily relies on staples such as potatoes, cabbage, and meat, modern chefs have started experimenting with a wider range of ingredients, including exotic spices, fine herbs, and locally sourced seasonal produce. This infusion of flavors adds a unique touch to classic dishes, transforming them into exciting culinary experiences.

Another important element of Modern Polish Flair is the presentation. Chefs are now paying special attention to the visual aspect of their creations, elevating traditional Polish dishes to works of art. This attention to detail not only enhances the dining experience but also establishes a connection between Polish cuisine and contemporary food trends.

Furthermore, modern techniques and cooking methods are being incorporated into traditional Polish recipes. Sous vide, molecular gastronomy, and other innovative cooking techniques are being used to create dishes with surprising textures and tastes, while still maintaining the essence of Polish culinary heritage. The blending of old and new techniques showcases the evolution and adaptability of Polish cuisine.

The importance of Modern Polish Flair lies in its ability to preserve and promote Polish culinary traditions while embracing innovation. By incorporating modern influences, Polish cuisine becomes more dynamic and accessible to a wider audience. It adds a level of excitement and intrigue, attracting both locals and tourists, and ensuring that Polish gastronomy remains relevant in a rapidly changing culinary landscape.

Modern Polish Flair has become an integral part of Polish cuisine, bringing new dimensions to traditional dishes. Through the creative use of ingredients, innovative techniques, and visually stunning presentations, it has successfully elevated Polish gastronomy to a whole new level. This culinary movement not only celebrates Poland's rich culinary heritage but also ensures its continued relevance in the global food scene.

14.1.1 Contemporary Polish Plating

Fusion Pierogi Creations play a significant role in the Polish cuisine. These innovative and unique dishes combine traditional Polish pierogi with flavors and ingredients from different cultures, resulting in a fusion of tastes that tantalize the palate.

One of the reasons why Fusion Pierogi Creations are important in Polish cuisine is that they showcase the diversity and adaptability of traditional Polish dishes. By incorporating ingredients and techniques from other culinary traditions, such as Asian or Mediterranean cuisine, Fusion Pierogi Creations introduce new and exciting flavors to the traditional Polish cuisine, making it more dynamic and appealing to a wider audience.

Furthermore, Fusion Pierogi Creations contribute to the evolution of Polish culinary traditions. Through experimentation and creativity, chefs and home cooks alike are able to create innovative pierogi fillings that push the boundaries of traditional flavors. This not only keeps the cuisine interesting and relevant but also attracts younger generations to appreciate and experiment with Polish cuisine.

Additionally, Fusion Pierogi Creations are important in promoting cultural exchange and understanding. By blending different culinary influences, these dishes create a bridge between cultures, showcasing the harmonious amalgamation of traditions. This brings people together and promotes an appreciation for diversity and multiculturalism.

Moreover, Fusion Pierogi Creations have gained popularity both domestically and internationally. These dishes have become a symbol of modern Polish cuisine and are often featured in culinary events, food festivals, and restaurants around the world. This recognition not only boosts the reputation of Polish cuisine but also enhances tourism and economic opportunities.

Fusion Pierogi Creations have emerged as an essential component of Polish cuisine. With their ability to combine traditional flavors with global influences, these dishes not only keep the cuisine exciting and relevant but also promote cultural exchange and understanding. Through their popularity and recognition, they have played a vital role in promoting Polish culinary traditions on a global scale.

14.1.2 Fusion Pierogi Creations

Fusion Pierogi Creations are a unique culinary innovation that combines traditional Polish pierogies with flavors and ingredients from various cuisines around the world. This fusion concept has gained popularity in recent years due to its ability to provide a fresh and exciting twist to a beloved classic.

One of the reasons why Fusion Pierogi Creations are so important is that they celebrate cultural diversity and bring people together through food. By incorporating elements from different culinary traditions, these creations allow individuals to experience new flavors and textures that they may not have been exposed to before. This not only expands their palate but also encourages them to embrace and appreciate different cultures.

Additionally, Fusion Pierogi Creations have a significant impact on the culinary industry. Chefs and restaurants that specialize in these innovative creations often receive recognition for their creativity and boldness. This not only brings attention to their establishments but also helps to elevate the overall perception and value of pierogies as a menu item. As a result, the demand for Fusion Pierogi Creations continues to grow, leading to a greater appreciation for the dish and its potential for culinary experimentation.

Furthermore, Fusion Pierogi Creations can be seen as a form of culinary art. Chefs approach these creations with an artistic mindset, using ingredients, colors, and presentation techniques to create visually stunning and gastronomically memorable dishes. This artistic element adds an extra dimension to the dining experience, transforming a simple dumpling into a work of culinary art that engages all the senses.

Fusion Pierogi Creations are of great importance due to their ability to celebrate cultural diversity, promote culinary innovation, and create an immersive dining experience. These creations have the power to bring people together, elevate the perception of pierogies, and showcase the artistic possibilities within the culinary world. By embracing the fusion concept, we can continue to explore new flavors, push culinary boundaries, and appreciate the richness of various cultures through a beloved and timeless dish.

Chapter 14.   Bringing It All Together

Polish cuisine is a perfect example of how the country's rich history and diverse cultural influences have shaped its culinary tradition. Over the centuries, Poland has been influenced by neighboring countries and foreign invaders, resulting in a vibrant and unique gastronomy that combines the best of Eastern and Western Europe.

One of the key aspects that brings everything together in Polish cuisine is the use of fresh and locally sourced ingredients. The Polish people take great pride in their agricultural resources, and the abundance of forests, rivers, and fertile lands ensures a steady supply of high-quality produce, meat, dairy, and grains. This emphasis on local ingredients is reflected in traditional Polish dishes, which often feature simple but delicious flavors.

A defining characteristic of Polish cuisine is the hearty nature of its dishes. Polish cuisine is known for its generous servings and rich flavors, making it perfect for cold winter days. Traditional meals often revolve around ingredients like potatoes, cabbage, pork, beef, and poultry, resulting in dishes that are both filling and satisfying.

Some of the most famous Polish dishes include pierogi, bigos, and gołąbki. Pierogi are savory dumplings often filled with ingredients such as potatoes, cheese, meat, or vegetables. They are typically boiled or fried and served with various toppings like sour cream or butter. Bigos, also known as hunter's stew, is a flavorful dish made from sauerkraut, fresh cabbage, and a variety of meats, such as pork, beef, or sausage. Gołąbki, or stuffed cabbage rolls, are another beloved Polish dish made from cabbage leaves filled with meat and rice, and then simmered in a flavorful tomato sauce.

Polish cuisine also incorporates a wide range of herbs and spices, further enhancing the flavors of the dishes. Popular seasonings include marjoram, parsley, dill, black pepper, and caraway seeds. These spices add depth and complexity to the traditional flavors, creating a delightful culinary experience.

Furthermore, Polish cuisine has been greatly influenced by religious and cultural traditions. For example, during Lent, when meat consumption is restricted, traditional Polish dishes often feature fish, potatoes, and dairy products. The festive season of Christmas is marked by the preparation of a special twelve-dish supper called Wigilia, where each dish symbolizes something different.

In recent years, Polish cuisine has also witnessed a modernization and fusion with international flavors. Chefs from Poland are incorporating new techniques and ingredients into their traditional recipes, resulting in innovative and exciting dishes that appeal to a wider audience.

The bringing together of various culinary influences, local produce, hearty flavors, and cultural traditions is what defines Polish cuisine. Whether it's the comforting and familiar taste of a traditional dish or the creative innovations of modern chefs, Polish cuisine continues to captivate food lovers around the world with its rich history and delicious flavors.

15.1 Hosting a Polish Feast

Hosting a Polish Feast is a celebration of Polish culture, traditions, and delicious cuisine. I will provide a detailed account of how to host a memorable and authentic Polish feast.

To begin, it is important to understand the significance of each dish in a traditional Polish feast. This feast usually starts with a variety of appetizers such as Pierogi, which are delicious dumplings filled with various savory fillings like potato, cheese, or meat. Another popular appetizer is Polskie ogórki, which are Polish pickles that add a tangy and crunchy element to the meal.

Moving on to the main course, a Polish feast often features a variety of meat dishes. One staple dish is Bigos, also known as Hunter's stew, which is a hearty combination of sauerkraut, different types of meat, and mushrooms. It is slow-cooked to perfection and is bursting with flavors. Another popular meat dish is Kotlet Schabowy, which is a Polish version of breaded pork chops, served with mashed potatoes and pickled cabbage.

In addition to the meat dishes, Polish feasts also include a wide selection of side dishes and salads. Kapusta, a traditional Polish sauerkraut, is often served as a side dish along with boiled potatoes. For salad lovers, Salata warzywna, a refreshing vegetable salad with a tangy dressing, is a perfect choice. It combines fresh veggies like cucumbers, tomatoes, and peppers, providing a burst of freshness to the feast.

No Polish feast is complete without a variety of desserts. Makowiec, a traditional poppy seed cake, is a popular choice. It is made with a rich and moist dough, filled with a sweet poppy seed paste, and rolled into a log shape. Another favorite dessert is Sernik, a Polish cheesecake with a dense and creamy texture. It is often flavored with vanilla or citrus zest, and served with a dollop of whipped cream.

To create an authentic atmosphere for your Polish feast, consider incorporating Polish decorations and music. Tablecloths with traditional designs, Polish folk art, and vibrant flowers can enhance the visual appeal. Playing traditional Polish music or having live musicians perform can create a lively and festive ambiance.

Lastly, consider organizing traditional Polish activities or games to engage your guests. Polka dancing, a popular Polish dance, can bring a lot of energy and fun to the feast. You can also include activities like piñata-breaking or a pierogi-eating contest to add excitement and laughter to the event.

Hosting a Polish feast is a wonderful way to celebrate the rich culture and delicious culinary heritage of Poland. By following the guidelines above and incorporating traditional elements, you can create a memorable and authentic experience for your guests. So gather your loved ones, embrace the Polish spirit, and enjoy the feast!

15.1.1 Planning Your Polish Menu

Polish cuisine is known for its hearty and flavorful dishes. When planning your Polish menu, it is important to consider a combination of traditional favorites and regional specialties. Here is a detailed guide you through the process.

Start by deciding on the number of courses you want to serve. Polish meals typically consist of multiple courses, including soup, appetizers, main courses, and desserts. For a complete dining experience, aim for at least three courses.

Next, choose an authentic Polish soup to kick off your meal. A popular choice is żurek, a sour rye soup made with fermented rye flour. Another option is barszcz, a vibrant beet soup that can be served hot or cold. Both soups are rich in flavor and will set the tone for your menu.

For appetizers, pierogi is a must-have. These dumplings are filled with various ingredients such as potato and cheese, sauerkraut and mushroom, or meat. Serve them boiled or fried, and offer a selection of dipping sauces like sour cream or melted butter.

Moving on to the main course, consider serving a traditional Polish dish like bigos. This hearty hunter's stew is made with sauerkraut, fresh cabbage, and an assortment of meats, such as sausages, bacon, and beef. It is slow-cooked to perfection and often enjoyed with a side of crusty bread.

Another delicious main course option is łazanki, a dish made with wide pasta noodles, cabbage, and bacon. It is commonly served with a dollop of sour cream and is a favorite among Polish cuisine enthusiasts.

Don't forget to include some classic side dishes. Kluski, which are Polish dumplings, can be served alongside the main course. These tasty dumplings are made with flour, potatoes, or semolina and can be boiled, fried, or baked.

To round out your menu, offer a variety of Polish desserts. Favorites include sernik, a creamy cheesecake, and makowiec, a poppy seed roll. Both are sweet treats that will leave your guests satisfied.

When planning your Polish menu, it is essential to consider the dietary preferences and restrictions of your guests. Provide vegetarian and gluten-free options to ensure there is something for everyone to enjoy.

Planning your Polish menu involves selecting a variety of courses and dishes that showcase the rich flavors and traditions of Polish cuisine. By including popular soups, appetizers, main courses, and desserts, you can create a memorable dining experience for your guests.

15.1.2 Setting the Table with Polish Flair

Setting the table with Polish flair entails combining elegance and tradition to create a visually pleasing and culturally rich dining experience. From the choice of tableware to the arrangement of items, each element plays a significant role in showcasing Polish heritage and hospitality. This will delve into the various aspects of setting the table with Polish flair, including the selection of tablecloth, dinnerware, glassware, flatware, and decorative elements.

Tablecloth:

Traditionally, Polish tablecloths are made from linen or lace to add a touch of sophistication to the dining experience. The color and pattern of the tablecloth should complement the overall theme of the table setting. Polish designs often feature intricate floral motifs or geometric patterns, reflecting the country's folk art heritage. It is essential to iron the tablecloth meticulously before setting it on the table to avoid any wrinkles or creases.

Dinnerware:

When setting the table with Polish flair, one should opt for high-quality porcelain or ceramic dinnerware. Polish pottery, known as "Bolesławiec Pottery" or "Polish Stoneware," is renowned worldwide for its vibrant colors and intricate hand-painted designs. The dinnerware often showcases traditional Polish patterns such as peacock feathers, floral motifs, or folk-inspired designs. Each plate, bowl, and serving dish should be carefully placed to ensure a visually appealing arrangement.

Glassware:

Glassware selection is crucial when setting the table with Polish flair. Crystal glasses are highly favored, as they exude elegance and reflect light beautifully. Polish crystal glassware is recognized for its exceptional clarity and craftsmanship. The collection may include wine glasses, water goblets, champagne flutes, and a variety of other glassware to cater to different beverages. Make sure to polish the glasses thoroughly before placing them on the table to enhance their sparkle.

Flatware:

In a traditional Polish table setting, stainless steel or silver flatware is commonly used. The cutlery should be polished to shine, reflecting the attention to detail. The table setting generally includes a dinner and salad fork, knife, soup spoon, and dessert spoon. Polish flatware often features decorative handles, such as ornate designs or intricate carvings, adding a touch of uniqueness to the dining experience.

Decorative Elements:

To complete the table setting with Polish flair, consider incorporating decorative elements that showcase Polish culture. This may include placing Polish folk art items, such as hand-painted ceramic figurines or wooden sculptures, as centerpieces. Additionally, fresh flowers arranged in Polish pottery vases can enhance the overall aesthetic appeal. Candles, preferably scented or with religious symbolism, can create a cozy and inviting atmosphere.

Setting the table with Polish flair involves carefully selecting and arranging various elements to create a culturally rich dining experience. From the choice of tablecloth and dinnerware to the selection of glassware and decorative elements, each component contributes to showcasing Polish heritage and hospitality. By paying attention to detail and incorporating traditional Polish elements, one can create a visually pleasing and memorable dining experience that reflects the elegance and charm of Polish culture.

RECIPES

Chapter 15.   Appetizers and Starters

1.   Classic Potato and Cheese Pierogi

Prep Time; One hour

Cook time; 20 minutes

Serves: 4-6 Serves

Ingredients:

- Two cups all-purpose flour
- One-half teaspoon salt
- One large egg
- One-half cup water
- Two cups mashed potatoes
- One cup grated cheddar cheese
- One-half teaspoon black pepper
- One-fourth cup unsalted butter
- One medium-sized onion, diced

Directions:

1. Flour and salt should be mixed together in a big bowl before use. Whisk the egg and water together in a separate bowl until combined. To make a dense dough, gradually add the egg mixture to the flour mixture while combining the two together thoroughly.

2. Knead the dough on a surface that has been dusted with flour for about five minutes, or until it is silky smooth and elastic. Ten minutes after covering the dough with a wet cloth, the dough should be allowed to rest.

3. Meanwhile, in a separate bowl, mix together the mashed potatoes, grated cheddar cheese, and black pepper.

4. On a surface dusted with flour, roll out the dough to a thickness of approximately one eight of an inch. To form circles from the dough, you can either make use of a round cookie cutter or a drinking glass.

5. Place a small spoonful of the potato filling onto each dough circle. Fold the dough in half, sealing the edges by pinching them together. Repeat this process with the remaining dough and filling.

6. Bring a large pot of salted water to a boil. Cook the pierogi in batches for about 5 minutes, or until they float to the surface. Remove them from the water with a slotted spoon and transfer them to a colander to drain.

7. Butter will be melted in a skillet over a heat setting of medium. After adding the sliced onion, continue cooking it until it turns translucent and just begins to brown.

8. Serve the pierogi hot, topped with the sautéed onions and additional butter if desired.

Nutrition: Calories (per serving): 350 calories Fat: 12g Carbs: 50g Protein: 10g

NOTES:
_____
_____
_____

2. Mushroom and Sauerkraut Pierogi

Prep Time; 30 minutes

Cook time; 20 minutes

Serves: 4

Ingredients:

- Two cups all-purpose flour
- One-half teaspoon salt
- One-half cup warm water
- One tablespoon vegetable oil
- One medium onion, finely chopped
- Two cups mushrooms, finely chopped
- One cup sauerkraut, drained and rinsed
- One-half tsp dried thyme
- Salt & pepper, as required
- Two tbsp butter

Directions:

1. Flour and salt should be mixed together in a big bowl. Mix while adding the warm water in a slow and steady stream until the dough begins to come together. Knead the dough for approximately five minutes, or until it is completely smooth. Allow it to sit undisturbed for ten minutes while you cover it with a damp cloth.

2. Warm the vegetable oil in a skillet over a heat setting somewhere in the middle. After adding the chopped onion, continue to heat for approximately 5 minutes, or until the onion has softened. Cook for an additional five minutes after adding the mushrooms and the sauerkraut. Add thyme, salt, and pepper to taste, and season with salt as well. Take it away from the heat and let it cool down some.

3. On a surface that has been dusted with flour, roll out the dough to a thickness of approximately one eight of an inch. Cut out circles of dough with a glass or a round cookie cutter to a diameter of about 3 inches (7.5 centimeters).

4. Each dough circle should have a heaping teaspoon of the mushroom and sauerkraut filling placed in the middle of it. Create a half-moon shape by folding the dough over the filling to cover it. To ensure a good seal, pinch the edges.

5. Start the cooking process by bringing a large pot of salted water to a boil. Pierogi should be added in batches and cooked for approximately five minutes, or until they rise to the surface of the water. Take them out using a slotted spoon, then place them on a plate.

6. Melt the butter in a separate pan over medium heat so it may be used later. After adding the cooked pierogi, sauté them for about two minutes on each side, or until they have a golden brown color.

7. Serve hot with sour cream or another sauce of your choosing as a dipping option.

Nutrition (per serving): Calories: 315 Fat: 9g Carbs: 50g Protein: 9g

NOTES:
_____
_____
_____

3. Borscht: The Jewel of Polish Soups

Prep Time; 15 minutes

Cook time; One hour

Serves: 4

Ingredients:

- Four medium beets, peeled and grated
- Two carrots, peeled and grated
- One onion, finely chopped
- Two cloves garlic, minced
- Four cups vegetable or beef broth
- Two cups shredded cabbage
- One can diced tomatoes
- One tablespoon tomato paste
- One bay leaf
- One teaspoon dried dill
- Salt and pepper to taste
- Sour cream for serving

Directions:

1. Put some oil into a big pot and cook it over medium heat. Add the garlic that has been minced and the chopped onion. Keep cooking until the onion loses its opaque quality.

2. Be sure to include the grated carrots and beets in the pot. Continue to stir occasionally while cooking for approximately 5 minutes.

3. The broth, either vegetable or beef, should be poured in and brought to a boil. Turn the heat down to low and let it simmer for half an hour.

4. Place the shredded cabbage, diced tomatoes, tomato paste, dried dill, pepper, salt, and bay leaf into the pot. Stir to combine. Make sure there are no lumps, then continue to boil for another half an hour.

5. Remove the bay leaf and taste the soup. Adjust the seasoning if needed.

6. To serve, dollop some sour cream on top while still hot.

Nutrition: Calories: 150 Fat: 5g Carbs: 20g Protein: 7g

NOTES:

_____
_____
_____

4. Pickled Herring Salad

Prep Time; 10 minutes

Cook time; 0 minutes

Serves: 4

Ingredients:

- One pound pickled herring fillets, drained and cut into small pieces
- One-half red onion, thinly sliced
- One-half cup sour cream
- One-fourth cup mayonnaise
- Two tbsp. Dijon mustard
- One tbsp. white wine vinegar
- Two tbsp fresh dill, chopped
- Salt & pepper, as required
- Rye bread or crackers, for serving

Directions:

1. Mix the herring that has been pickled, the red onion, the sour cream, the mayonnaise, the Dijon mustard, the white wine vinegar, and the fresh dill in a big bowl. Be sure to blend everything thoroughly.

2. Season with salt and pepper to taste. Refrigerate for at least One hour to allow the flavors to meld together.

3. Serve the pickled herring salad on rye bread or crackers. Enjoy!

Nutrition: Calories: 220 Fat: 12g Carbs: 7g Protein: 20g

NOTES:

_____
_____
_____

5. Tatar: Polish Herring Tartare

Prep Time; 15 minutes

Cook time; 0 minutes

Serves: 4

Ingredients:

- 200g Polish herring fillets
- One small red onion, finely chopped
- Two pickles, finely chopped
- Two tbsp. capers, chopped
- Two tbsp fresh dill, chopped
- Two tbsp fresh parsley, chopped
- Two tbsp lemon juice
- Two tbsp extra virgin olive oil
- Salt & pepper, as required

Directions:

1. After being washed in ice-cold water, the herring fillets should be dried off using a paper towel.

2. Herring fillets should be chopped very finely before being placed in a mixing dish.

3. In a bowl, combine the chopped red onion, pickles, capers, dill, and parsley. Add the herring to the dish.

4. The lemon juice, olive oil, salt, and pepper should be mixed together in a small bowl using a whisk.

5. After pouring the dressing over the herring mixture, mix everything together using a light hand.

6. Refrigerate the bowl, covered with plastic wrap, for at least an hour, so that the flavors can combine and become more pronounced.

7. Serve the Tatar: Polish Herring Tartare chilled, garnished with additional fresh herbs if desired.

Nutrition: Calories: 220 Fat: 14g Carbs: 8g Protein: 15g

NOTES:

6. Paszteciki: Polish Pastry Pockets

Prep Time; One hour

Cook time; 30 minutes

Serves: 12

Ingredients:

For the dough:

- Two cups all-purpose flour
- One-half tsp. salt
- One-half cup unsalted butter, cold and cubed
- One-half cup sour cream

For the filling:

- One cup cooked chicken, finely chopped
- One small onion, finely chopped
- Two tbsp. vegetable oil
- One-half teaspoon dried thyme
- Salt & pepper, as required

For the egg wash:

- One egg, beaten

Directions:

1. Flour and salt should be mixed together in a big bowl before use. Utilizing either a pastry cutter or your fingers, cut the butter into the dry ingredients until the mixture resembles coarse crumbs.

2. Mix the dough while adding the sour cream and continuing to do so until it comes together. Make a ball out of the dough, wrap it in plastic wrap, and place it in the refrigerator for half an hour.

3. Warm the vegetable oil in a skillet over a heat setting somewhere in the middle. After adding the onion, continue cooking it until it becomes translucent. Include some chopped chicken, some dried thyme, some salt, and some pepper in the dish. Continue cooking for another five minutes, after which take it off the fire and let it cool.

4. Prepare a baking sheet by lining it with parchment paper and heating the oven to 375 degrees Fahrenheit (190 degrees Celsius).

5. On a surface dusted with flour, roll out the dough to a thickness of approximately one eight of an inch. Use a glass or a cookie cutter to make holes in the shape of circles.

6. Each dough circle should have a heaping teaspoon of the chicken filling placed in the middle of it. To seal the filling within, fold the dough over it and crimp the sides together.

7. Move the filled pockets to the baking sheet that has been previously prepared. Coat the tops with the egg that has been beaten.

8. Bake for 25 to 30 minutes, or until a golden brown color has developed.

9. After removing the paszteciki from the oven, allow them to cool for a couple of minutes before serving.

Nutrition: Calories: 220 per serving Fat: 14g Carbs: 18g Protein: 7g

NOTES:

_____
_____
_____

7. Barszcz and Its Variations

Prep Time; 20 minutes

Cook time; 2 hours

Serves: 4

Ingredients:

- Four medium beets, peeled and grated
- One onion, finely chopped
- Four cups vegetable broth
- Two carrots, peeled and grated
- Two potatoes, peeled and diced
- One clove garlic, minced
- One tablespoon tomato paste
- Two tablespoons white vinegar
- Salt and pepper, to taste
- Sour cream, for garnish
- Fresh dill, for garnish

Directions:

1. Put the grated beets, the chopped onion, and the vegetable broth in a large pot. Stir to combine. Bring to a boil, then immediately reduce the heat and simmer for approximately one hour, or until the beets are soft.

2. Put into the saucepan the carrots that have been grated, potatoes that have been diced, garlic that has been minced, and tomato paste. After giving it a good stir, continue to simmer it for another half an hour, or until the vegetables are completely cooked.

3. After stirring in the white vinegar, season the mixture to taste with salt and pepper. Take the pot off the heat.

4. Before serving, the barszcz should be allowed to come to room temperature. The soup should be served in bowls and topped with a dollop of sour cream and some fresh dill for garnish.

Nutrition: Calories: 180 Fat: 2g Carbs: 38g Protein: 5g

NOTES:

_____
_____
_____

8. Placki Ziemniaczane: Potato Pancakes

Prep Time; 15 minutes

Cook time; 20 minutes

Serves: 4

Ingredients:

- Four large potatoes, peeled
- One onion, grated
- Two eggs, beaten
- Four tbsp. all-purpose flour
- One teaspoon salt
- One-half teaspoon pepper
- Vegetable oil for frying

Directions:

1. Grate the peeled potatoes into a large bowl.

2. Add the grated onion to the bowl.

3. Using a clean kitchen towel, squeeze out any excess moisture from the potato-onion mixture.

4. In a bowl, combine the eggs that have been beaten with the flour, salt, and pepper. Be sure to blend everything thoroughly.

5. Prepare the sauce in a large frying pan by heating the vegetable oil over medium heat.

6. Drop spoonfuls of the potato mixture into the hot oil, flattening them slightly with the back of the spoon.

7. Fry the potato pancakes for approximately five minutes per side, or until they are golden brown and crispy.

8. Take the fried pancakes out of the pan and let them drain on some paper towels to get rid of the excess oil.

9. Serve the Placki Ziemniaczane hot with sour cream or applesauce.

Nutrition (per serving): Calories: 250 Fat: 10g Carbs: 35g Protein: 6g

NOTES:

_____
_____
_____

9. *Pyzy: Potato Dumplings*

Prep Time; 30 minutes

Cook time; 30 minutes

Serves: 4

Ingredients:

- Four large potatoes, peeled and boiled
- One cup all-purpose flour
- One tsp salt
- One-half tsp black pepper
- One-half onion, finely chopped
- Two tbsp. vegetable oil
- Sour cream, for serving

Directions:

1. Mash the boiled potatoes until smooth in a large mixing bowl.

2. Add flour, salt, and black pepper to the mashed potatoes. Mix well to form a dough.

3. On a surface that has been dusted with flour only gently, roll the dough into a log form. Reduce the timber to pieces no larger than one inch in width.

4. Take each piece and roll it into a ball. Use your thumb to make an indentation in the center of each ball.

5. Fill the indentation with a small amount of chopped onion.

6. Start the boiling process for a large pot of salted water. After about ten to twelve minutes, or until the dumplings float to the surface, add the dumplings and continue cooking.

7. Drain the dumplings and set aside.

8. In a saucepan, bring the oil from the veggie to a medium heat. After the dumplings have finished cooking, add them to the pan and sauté them over low heat until they are golden brown.

9. Take the dumplings made with pyzy off the burner and serve them hot with sour cream.

Nutrition: Calories: 250 Fat: 7g Carbs: 40g Protein: 6g

NOTES:

_____
_____
_____

10. Kaszanka: Blood Sausage

Prep Time; 20 minutes

Cook time; 40 minutes

Serves: 4

Ingredients:

- One lb pork liver
- One lb pork blood
- One lb pork fatback
- One cup buckwheat groats
- One onion, finely chopped
- 2 cloves garlic, minced
- One tsp. marjoram
- One tsp. salt
- One-half tsp. black pepper
- 1/4 tsp. allspice

Directions:

1. Cook the buckwheat groats according to package instructions. Set aside.

2. Start by heating some oil in a big skillet over a medium flame. Cook the chopped onion and garlic in the minced garlic until the onion becomes transparent.

3. In a food processor, grind the pork liver, pork fatback, and buckwheat groats until well combined.

4. Mix the pork blood with the ground meat mixture in a big bowl. The bowl should be used for mixing. Combine thoroughly by thoroughly mixing.

5. Add the onion and garlic mixture that has been sautéed to the bowl. Marjoram, salt, black pepper, and allspice should be used as seasonings. Combine completely.

6. After lining a loaf pan with parchment paper, pour in the batter and pat it down firmly to ensure that it is evenly distributed.

7. Set the temperature in the oven to 350 degrees Fahrenheit (175 degrees Celsius). Bake the bread in the oven for forty minutes, or until the internal temperature reaches 160 degrees Fahrenheit (71 degrees Celsius), whichever comes first.

8. Before removing the kaszanka from the loaf pan, give it a few minutes to cool down significantly. It should be cut into substantial servings.

Nutrition (per serving): Calories: 320 Fat: 20g Carbs: 10g Protein: 25g

Chapter 16.   Soups That Warm the Soul

11. Żurek: Sour Rye Soup

Prep Time; 20 minutes

Cook time; 2 hours

Serves: 6

Ingredients:

- 500g sour rye flour
- 200g smoked bacon, diced
- One large onion, chopped
- Two cloves of garlic, minced
- Two bay leaves
- Five allspice berries
- One teaspoon marjoram
- Three medium potatoes, peeled and diced
- One tablespoon vegetable oil
- One cup sour cream
- Salt and pepper to taste
- Fresh parsley for garnish

Directions:

1. Put the sour rye flour in a big pot and cover it with water. Stir occasionally. Allow it to sit out for a full day to ferment.

2. Fry the bacon in a separate pan until it's nice and crispy. Take the bacon out of the pan and set it aside somewhere else.

3. Put the chopped onion and garlic that has been minced into the same pan. Sauté the onion until it reaches a transparent state.

4. Add the sautéed onion and garlic to the pot with the fermented sour rye flour. Also, add the bay leaves, allspice berries, marjoram, and diced potatoes.

5. Bring the mixture to a boil, then reduce the heat and let it simmer for 1.5-2 hours, or until the potatoes are tender.

6. In a small pan, heat the vegetable oil and fry the reserved crispy bacon until it becomes crunchy. Set it aside for later.

7. Once the soup is cooked, remove the bay leaves and allspice berries. Stir in the sour cream and season with salt and pepper to taste.

8. Serve the Żurek garnished with the crispy bacon and fresh parsley.

Nutrition (Per Serving): Calories: 350 Fat: 15g Carbs: 40g Protein: 15g

NOTES:
_____
_____
_____

12. Rosół: Polish Chicken Soup

Prep Time; 15 minutes

Cook time; One hour 30 minutes

Serves: 6

Ingredients:

- One whole chicken (about 3-4 pounds)
- Eight cups water
- One onion, peeled and quartered
- Two carrots, peeled and sliced
- Two celery stalks, sliced
- Two parsnips, peeled and sliced
- One leek, sliced
- Two cloves garlic, minced
- Two bay leaves
- One teaspoon whole peppercorns
- Salt, to taste
- Fresh parsley, chopped (for garnish)

Directions:

1. Put the chicken in a big pot and add enough water to cover it completely. Bring to a boil, then remove any froth that forms on the surface by skimming it off.

2. Add the onion, carrots, celery, parsnips, leek, garlic, bay leaves, and peppercorns to the pot.

3. Turn the heat down to a low setting and let the mixture boil for one hour, scraping out any contaminants that float to the surface.

4. After an hour, take the chicken out of the pot and put it somewhere else so it can finish cooling down. After the meat has had time to cool, separate it from the bones, and then shred it into pieces that are easily digestible. Throw away the skin as well as the bones.

5. Return the shredded chicken to the pot and continue simmering for another 30 minutes.

6. Season with salt to taste.

7. Serve hot, garnished with fresh parsley.

Nutrition:

Calories: 250 per serving Fat: 10g Carbs: 10g Protein: 30g

13. Kapuśniak: Cabbage Soup

Prep Time; 15 minutes

Cook time; One hour 30 minutes

Serves: 4-6

Ingredients:

- One large head of cabbage, shredded
- One onion, diced
- Two carrots, sliced
- Two potatoes, cubed
- Four cups vegetable broth
- Two cups water
- One can (14 oz) diced tomatoes
- One bay leaf
- One tsp dried marjoram
- One tsp dried thyme
- Salt and pepper to taste
- Sour cream for serving (optional)

Directions:

1. Start by warming some oil in a big saucepan set over medium heat. After adding the onion and carrots, continue to sauté them for approximately 5 minutes, or until they begin to soften.

2. After adding the shredded cabbage and continuing to sauté for an additional 5 minutes, the cabbage should start to wilt.

3. Mix in the chopped tomatoes, vegetable broth, water, bay leaf, and dried herbs of your choice (we used marjoram, thyme, and marjoram). Bring the soup up to the boiling point.

4. Turn the burner down to a low setting, cover the pot, and let the mixture simmer for one hour while stirring it occasionally.

5. After adding the potatoes in cubes, continue to simmer for another half an hour, or until the potatoes are fork-tender.

6. The bay leaf should be removed, and the soup should be seasoned to taste with salt and pepper.

7. Serve hot and top each bowl with a dollop of sour cream if desired.

Nutrition: Calories: 200 per serving Fat: 4g Carbs: 40g Protein: 6g

14. Karp Po Żydowsku: Jewish-Style Carp

Prep Time; 30 minutes

Cook time; 45 minutes

Serves: 4

Ingredients:

- One whole carp (about 2-3 pounds), cleaned and scaled
- One onion, chopped
- Two cloves garlic, minced
- Twp tbsp. vegetable oil
- One cup tomato sauce
- One cup fish stock or vegetable broth
- One tsp. paprika
- One tsp. dried marjoram
- One tsp. dried thyme
- Salt & pepper, as required
- Fresh parsley, chopped for garnish

Directions:

1. Set the temperature in the oven to 375 degrees Fahrenheit (190 degrees Celsius).

2. To preheat the vegetable oil, place it in a large oven-safe pan or baking dish and set the heat to medium. Sauté the chopped onion and garlic until it becomes soft and translucent, then add it to the pan with the rest of the ingredients.

3. Place the cleaned and scaled carp in the skillet or baking dish. Add the tomato sauce and fish stock or vegetable broth.

4. Sprinkle the paprika, dried marjoram, dried thyme, salt, and pepper over the carp. Mix well to ensure the seasonings are evenly distributed.

5. Cover the skillet or baking dish with foil and place it in the preheated oven. Bake for 30 minutes.

6. After thirty minutes, take off the aluminum foil and baste the carp with the liquid that has been cooking. Carp should be cooked all the way through and easily flake apart when tested with a fork after being returned to the oven after being baked uncovered for an additional 15 minutes.

7. Once cooked, remove the carp from the oven and let it rest for a few minutes.

8. Serve the carp hot, garnished with fresh chopped parsley.

Nutrition: Calories: 250 per serving Fat: 10g Carbs: 5g Protein: 35g

15. Łosoś z Sosem Koperkowym: Salmon with Dill Sauce

Prep Time; 15 minutes

Cook time; 20 minutes

Serves: 4

Ingredients:

- Four salmon fillets (about 6 ounces each)
- Salt & pepper, as required
- Two tbsp. olive oil
- One-half cup chicken broth
- One-half cup heavy cream
- Two tbsp. fresh dill, chopped
- Two tsp. lemon juice

Directions:

1. Salt and pepper should be applied to both sides of the salmon fillets before cooking.

2. In a large skillet, bring the olive oil up to temperature over medium heat.

3. Place the salmon fillets in the skillet and cook for approximately 4-5 minutes per side, or until the fish is cooked to the degree of doneness that you choose. Take the salmon out of the pan, and place it to the side.

4. In the same skillet, pour in the chicken broth and bring it to a simmer. Cook for 2-3 minutes to reduce the broth slightly.

5. In a skillet over medium heat, combine the heavy cream, fresh dill, and lemon juice. Mix to ensure a complete blending.

6. Continue to cook the sauce for an additional two to three minutes, or until it attains the desired level of thickness.

7. After you have returned the salmon fillets to the pan, spread some of the sauce over them. Continue cooking for one more minute to gently rewarm the salmon.

8. Serve the Salmon with Dill Sauce immediately, garnished with extra fresh dill, if desired.

Nutrition (per serving): Calories: 395 Fat: 29g Carbs: 2g Protein: 33g

NOTES:

_____
_____
_____

16. Kapusta kiszona z Grzybami: Sauerkraut Soup with Mushrooms

Prep Time; 15 minutes

Cook time; 45 minutes

Serves: 4

Ingredients:

- 500g sauerkraut, rinsed and drained
- 200g mushrooms, sliced
- One onion, diced
- Two cloves of garlic, minced
- Two tbsp. vegetable oil
- One bay leaf
- One tsp. dried marjoram
- One tsp. caraway seeds
- Four cups vegetable broth
- One cup water
- Salt & pepper, as required
- Sour cream and fresh dill for serving

Directions:

1. In a big pot, bring the vegetable oil to a temperature of medium heat. When the onion is transparent, add the garlic that has been minced and continue to cook.

2. When the mushrooms have released their moisture and begun to brown, add them to the pot and continue to simmer until they are done.

3. Stir in the sauerkraut, bay leaf, dried marjoram, and caraway seeds. Cook for a few minutes to combine the flavors.

4. Add the water and the veggie broth to the pot. Bring the soup to a boil, then lower the heat and let it simmer for around half an hour.

5. Salt and pepper can be added to taste as a seasoning.

6. Serve while still hot, garnishing each portion with a dollop of sour cream and a sprinkling of fresh dill.

Nutrition: Calories: 200 per serving Fat: 10g Carbs: 20g Protein: 8g

NOTES:

17. Chłodnik: Cold Beet Soup

Prep Time; 20 minutes

Cook time; 10 minutes

Serves: 4

Ingredients:

- Four medium beets, boiled, peeled, and grated
- One cucumber, peeled and grated
- Two cups plain yogurt
- One cup kefir
- One cup water
- Two green onions, finely chopped
- One small bunch fresh dill, finely chopped
- One tablespoon fresh lemon juice
- Salt, to taste
- Sugar, to taste
- Hard-boiled eggs, sliced (for garnish)
- Fresh dill sprigs (for garnish)

Directions:

1. Combine the grated beets, cucumber, yogurt, kefir, water, green onions, dill, lemon juice, and salt and sugar in a large mixing basin. Mix well.

2. Taste the dish, and make any necessary adjustments to the amount of salt and sugar. Keep in mind that the soup need to have a flavor that is a little bit sweet and a little bit sour.

3. Cover the bowl and refrigerate for at least 2 hours or overnight to let the flavors meld together.

4. Before serving, give the soup a stir. If it is too thick, you can add more water or kefir to reach your desired consistency.

5. Ladle the cold beet soup into serving bowls. Garnish with sliced hard-boiled eggs and fresh dill sprigs.

6. Serve chilled and enjoy!

Nutrition Calories: 180 Fat: 7g Carbs: 20g Protein: 10g

NOTES:

_____
_____
_____

18. Krem z Pieczonych Buraków: Cream of Roasted Beet Soup

Prep Time; 20 minutes

Cook time; One hour

Serves: 4

Ingredients:

- Four medium beets, roasted and peeled
- One small onion, chopped
- Two cloves of garlic, minced
- Two cups vegetable broth
- One cup heavy cream
- Salt and pepper to taste
- Fresh dill, for garnish

Directions:

1. Turn the temperature on the oven to 400 degrees Fahrenheit (200 degrees Celsius). Be sure to wrap the beets in aluminum foil before placing them in the oven. Roast them for about 45 to 60 minutes, or until they are soft. After allowing them to cool, peel them and cut them into small cubes.

2. Warm a few tablespoons of olive oil in a big saucepan set over a medium heat. Sauté the garlic that has been minced and the onion that has been chopped until the onion becomes transparent and softer.

3. Be sure to give the saucepan a good swirl after adding the roasted beets so that they can mingle with the onion and garlic. Continue to cook for one or two minutes more.

4. The vegetable broth should then be poured in and the pot should be brought to a boil. Turn the heat down to low and continue simmering the beets for approximately 15 minutes, or until they are very soft.

5. You can use a conventional blender or an immersion blender to purée the soup until it is completely smooth and creamy. Put the soup back into the original pot

6. After incorporating the heavy cream, season it to taste with salt and pepper. Warm the soup thoroughly over a low heat until it is ready to serve.

7. Serve the cream of roasted beet soup in bowls, garnished with fresh dill. Enjoy!

Nutrition Information (per serving): Calories: 240 Fat: 16g Carbs: 22g Protein: 4g

NOTES:

_____
_____
_____

19. Czernina: Duck Blood Soup

Prep Time; 20 minutes

Cook time; 2 hours

Serves: 4

Ingredients:

- One duck, cut into pieces
- One onion, chopped
- 2 cloves garlic, minced
- One cup duck blood
- One cup chicken broth
- One tablespoon red wine vinegar
- One tablespoon honey
- One bay leaf
- One-half teaspoon dried marjoram
- Salt and pepper to taste

Directions:

1. Cook the duck pieces in a large pot over medium-high heat until they have a browned appearance. Take the duck out of the way, and set it aside.

2. Sauté the garlic and onion in the same pot until the onion is translucent.

3. Place the duck back into the pot, then add the duck blood, chicken broth, red wine vinegar, honey, a bay leaf, marjoram, and a pinch each of salt and pepper. Stir to combine.

4. Bring the soup to a boil, then reduce the heat and let it simmer uncovered for about 2 hours, or until the duck is tender.

5. Skim off any impurities that rise to the surface during cooking.

6. After removing the duck pieces from the broth, the meat should be shredded. Throw away the skeletons and put the meat back into the stew pot.

7. Adjust the seasoning if needed.

8. Serve the Czernina hot with slices of bread or dumplings.

Nutrition: Calories: 250 per serving Fat: 10g Carbs: 15g Protein: 25g

NOTES:

_____
_____
_____

20. Kwas Chlebowy: Kvass Soup

Prep Time; 15 minutes

Cook time; One hour

Serves: 4

Ingredients:

- 500g beef, cubed
- One onion, chopped
- 3 carrots, diced
- Two potatoes, cubed
- 200g sauerkraut, rinsed
- One bay leaf
- One-liter kvass
- Salt & pepper, as required

Directions:

1. Put the steak into a big pot and cover it with water all the way around. Bring to a boil, then reduce heat and simmer for half an hour.

2. Remove any foam that forms on the surface.

3. The pot should now contain chopped onion, diced carrots, cubed potatoes, sauerkraut that has been rinsed, and a bay leaf. Add little salt and pepper before serving.

4. Kvass will now be added, and the soup will be brought to a boil.

5. Turn down the heat and let it simmer for another half an hour, or until the vegetables are cooked through.

6. Remove the bay leaf before serving.

Nutrition: Calories: 250 per serving Fat: 10g Carbs: 20g Protein: 20g

NOTES:

_____
_____
_____

Chapter 17. Hearty Meat Dishes:

21. Bigos: The Hunter's Stew

Prep Time; 30 minutes

Cook time; 3 hours

Serves: 6-8

Ingredients:

- 500g sauerkraut
- 500g fresh cabbage, shredded
- 250g smoked bacon, diced
- 250g Polish sausage, sliced
- 250g pork shoulder, cubed
- 250g beef stew meat, cubed
- One onion, chopped
- Two cloves garlic, minced
- Two bay leaves
- One teaspoon caraway seeds
- One teaspoon paprika
- One teaspoon dried marjoram
- Salt and pepper to taste
- Twooog dried mushrooms, soaked and chopped
- Two tablespoons tomato paste
- Two cups beef broth
- One cup red wine
- Two apples, peeled and sliced

Directions:

1. In a big pot, preheat it over medium heat, then add the bacon that has been diced. Cook until the meat is browned and crisp, then take it from the pot and set it aside.

2. Place the sliced Polish sausage, pork shoulder, and beef stew meat in the same saucepan and cook over medium heat. Cook until browned on all sides throughout the process. Take out of the cooking saucepan and leave aside.

3. Put the chopped onion and garlic that has been minced into the same pot. Cook until the vegetables are tender and aromatic.

4. To the pot, add the shredded cabbage, sauerkraut, bay leaves, caraway seeds, paprika, dried marjoram, salt, and pepper. Mix to ensure a complete blending.

5. The dried mushrooms should be soaked in water and then diced before being added to the saucepan along with tomato paste, beef broth, and red wine. Once again, stir in order to mix.

6. Return the cooked bacon, Polish sausage, pork shoulder, and beef stew meat to the pot. Stir everything together.

7. The stew should be simmered with the lid on the pot over low heat for two hours, with stirring every so often.

8. After two hours, add the sliced apples to the saucepan and continue to simmer the mixture for another hour with the lid off.

9. Adjust the seasoning if needed. Remove the bay leaves before serving.

Nutrition: (Per serving) Calories: 350 Fat: 15g Carbs: 20g Protein: 30g

NOTES:

_____
_____
_____

22. Kotlet Schabowy: Polish Pork Cutlet

Prep Time; 15 minutes

Cook time; 20 minutes

Serves: 4

Ingredients:

- Four boneless pork chops
- One cup all-purpose flour
- Two eggs, beaten
- One cup breadcrumbs
- Salt and pepper to taste
- Vegetable oil for frying

Directions:

1. Flatten the pork chops slightly with a meat mallet.

2. Salt and pepper should be applied to both sides of the pork chops before cooking.

3. Set up three shallow dishes. Place the flour in the first dish, beaten eggs in the second dish, and breadcrumbs in the third dish.

4. Flour each pork chop, then dip it into the egg mixture that has been beaten, and then coat it with breadcrumbs, pressing down firmly to ensure that they stick.

5. In a large skillet, bring the vegetable oil to a simmer over medium heat.

6. Fry the pork chops in the coating until the coating is golden brown and the pork chops are crispy, about 4-5 minutes per side.

7. Remove the pork chops from the skillet and drain on paper towels to remove excess oil.

8. Serve the Kotlet Schabowy hot with your favorite side dishes.

Nutrition (per serving): Calories: 450 Fat: 20g Carbs: 30g Protein: 35g

NOTES:

23. Gołąbki: Stuffed Cabbage Rolls

Prep Time; 30 minutes

Cook time; One hour

Serves: 6

Ingredients:

- One large head of cabbage
- One lb ground beef
- One-half cup cooked rice
- One small onion, finely chopped
- One clove garlic, minced
- One-half teaspoon salt
- One-fourtgh tsp. black pepper
- One can (14.5 oz) diced tomatoes, undrained
- One can (8 oz) tomato sauce
- One tbsp. brown sugar
- One tbsp. Worcestershire sauce

Directions:

1. Turn the temperature on the oven to 350 degrees Fahrenheit (175 degrees Celsius).

2. Start the boiling process with a large saucepan of water. Cook the cabbage for about five minutes, or until the outer leaves are tender enough to be easily peeled off, after which you should add the entire head of cabbage. Take the cabbage out of the pot and peel off 12 of the larger leaves in a cautious manner. Remove the large vein running through the middle of each leaf.

3. Mix the ground beef, rice that has been cooked, onion, garlic, salt, and black pepper together in a large mixing basin. Mix well.

4. Put a dollop of the meat mixture in the middle of each cabbage leaf and serve. While you are rolling up the leaf, tuck the sides in as you go. In a baking dish, arrange the rolls with the seam side down.

5. The chopped tomatoes, tomato sauce, brown sugar, and Worcestershire sauce should each be combined in their own bowl before proceeding. The rolls of cabbage should be covered in the sauce.

6. Bake for forty-five minutes with the baking dish covered in aluminum foil. Take off the aluminum foil and continue baking for another 15 minutes, or until the cabbage rolls are cooked all the way through and the sauce is bubbling.

7. Serve the Gołąbki hot with some of the sauce spooned over the top.

Nutrition (per serving): Calories: 348 Fat: 19g Carbs: 21g Protein: 24g

24. Kielbasa and Sauerkraut Rolls

Prep Time; 15 minutes

Cook time; 25 minutes

Serves: 4

Ingredients:

- One package of Kielbasa sausage (about 500g)
- One cup sauerkraut
- One tbsp. olive oil
- One medium onion, sliced
- One tsp. caraway seeds
- Salt & pepper, as required
- Four hot dog buns

Directions:

1. Turn the temperature on the oven to 400 degrees Fahrenheit (200 degrees Celsius).

2. Slice the Kielbasa sausage into 4 equal parts.

3. The olive oil should be heated up in a big skillet over a medium heat. After adding the sliced onion, continue cooking for about 5 minutes, or until the onion is tender and has a mild caramelization.

4. Add the caraway seeds to the skillet and stir for another minute.

5. Add the sauerkraut to the skillet and cook for 2-3 minutes, stirring occasionally.

6. Add some salt and pepper to the kimchi and sauerkraut mixture, and season it to your liking.

7. Lay the hot dog buns on a baking sheet. Place a slice of Kielbasa sausage on each bun.

8. Divide the sauerkraut mixture equally among the hot dog buns, spreading it on top of the Kielbasa.

9. Bake the Kielbasa and Sauerkraut Rolls in the preheated oven for about 15-20 minutes until the sausages are heated through and the buns are toasted.

10. Serve hot and enjoy!

Nutrition: Calories: 456 per serving Fat: 24g Carbs: 37g Protein: 20g

NOTES:

_____
_____
_____

25. Polskie Kopytka: Polish Potato Dumplings

Prep Time; 30 minutes

Cook time; 20 minutes

Serves: 4

Ingredients:

- 500 grams potatoes, peeled and boiled
- 200 grams all-purpose flour
- One egg
- Salt to taste
- Optional: 2 tablespoons breadcrumbs

Directions:

1. In a large mixing bowl, mash the boiled potatoes until they reach a smooth consistency.

2. Add the flour, egg, and salt to the mashed potatoes. Mix well until all the ingredients are combined.

3. Knead the dough until it becomes elastic and doesn't stick to your hands. If the dough is too sticky, gradually add a little more flour.

4. Cut the dough into several smaller pieces, and then roll each piece into the shape of a long rope.

5. Small segments of the rope, approximately 2 centimeters in length, should be cut from the rope.

6. Optional step: Roll each dumpling piece in breadcrumbs for an extra crispy texture.

7. Start the cooking process by bringing a large pot of salted water to a boil. Put the dumplings into the water that is already boiling, and cook them for approximately three to five minutes, or until they float to the surface.

8. Put the dumplings that have been cooked into a serving dish by using a slotted spoon.

Nutrition (per serving): Calories: 200 Fat: 1g Carbs: 40g Protein: 5g

NOTES:

_____
_____
_____

26. Jellied Pig's Feet

Prep Time; 30 minutes

Cook time; 4 hours

Serves: 6

Ingredients:

- Two pig's feet, cleaned and cut into small pieces
- One onion, chopped
- Two cloves of garlic, minced
- Eight ounces of mushrooms, sliced
- Two bay leaves
- One tsp. of black peppercorns
- One tsp. of salt
- One-half tsp. of dried thyme
- Four cups of water
- Two envelopes of unflavored gelatin

Directions:

1. In a large pot, add the pig's feet, onion, garlic, mushrooms, bay leaves, black peppercorns, salt, and dried thyme.

2. Pour the water into the pot, then place it over high heat so that it may come to a boil. As soon as it reaches a boil, turn the heat down to a low simmer and let it cook for three to four hours, or until the pig's feet are soft and the flavors have merged together.

3. Remove the pot from the heat and strain the liquid, discarding the solids. Let the liquid cool slightly.

4. In a separate bowl, dissolve the gelatin in cold water according to the package instructions.

5. Stir the dissolved gelatin into the liquid, making sure it is well combined.

6. Pour the mixture into individual molds or a large mold if preferred.

7. Keep the jelly in the refrigerator for at least six hours, or overnight, until it has reached the desired consistency.

8. To serve, dip the mold briefly in hot water to loosen the jelly. Carefully invert the mold onto a serving platter, and the jelly should slide out.

9. Slice the jellied pig's feet with mushrooms and serve chilled.

Nutrition (per serving): Calories: 220 Fat: 14g Carbs: 4g Protein: 18g

27. Kiełbasa Myśliwska: Hunter's Sausage

Prep Time; 20 minutes

Cook time; 30 minutes

Serves: 4-6 Serves

Ingredients:

- 500g Kiełbasa sausage
- One onion, finely chopped
- Two cloves garlic, minced
- Two tablespoons vegetable oil
- Two teaspoons paprika
- One teaspoon dried marjoram
- One-half tsp. black pepper
- One-fourth tsp. salt
- One-fourth cup water

Directions:

1. Slice the Kiełbasa sausage into bite-sized pieces.

2. Prepare the vegetable oil in a big skillet by heating it up over medium heat.

3. When the onion and garlic have reached the desired degree of tenderness, remove from the heat.

4. After the sausage has been sliced, add it to the skillet and cook it until it is browned.

5. On top of the sausage, evenly distribute the paprika, dried marjoram, cracked black pepper, and salt. Mix thoroughly to evenly coat.

6. After adding the water to the pan, give everything a good swirl to blend. Turn the heat down to a low setting and let it simmer for 15 minutes while stirring it occasionally.

7. Serve hot with the condiments and accompaniments of your choice.

Nutrition:

Calories (per serving): 300 Fat: 20g Carbs: 5g Protein: 25g

NOTES:

_____

_____

_____

28. Polish Meatballs (Klopsiki)

Prep Time; 20 minutes

Cook time; 30 minutes

Serves: 4

Ingredients:

- 500g ground beef
- One small onion, grated
- Two cloves garlic, minced
- One-half cup breadcrumbs
- One-fourth cup milk
- One egg
- One tablespoon chopped fresh parsley
- One teaspoon salt
- One-half teaspoon black pepper
- One-half teaspoon paprika
- One-fourth teaspoon ground nutmeg
- One-fourth teaspoon dried marjoram
- One-fourth teaspoon dried thyme
- One-fourth cup flour (for coating)
- Two tablespoons vegetable oil (for frying)

Directions:

1. In a large bowl, mix together ground beef, grated onion, minced garlic, breadcrumbs, milk, egg, parsley, salt, black pepper, paprika, nutmeg, marjoram, and thyme. Combine well until all ingredients are evenly incorporated.

2. Shape the mixture into small meatballs, about one inch in diameter.

3. Roll each meatball in flour to coat lightly.

4. Heat vegetable oil in a large skillet over medium heat. Add the meatballs in batches and cook until browned on all sides, about 8-10 minutes.

5. Once cooked, transfer the meatballs to a plate lined with paper towels to remove excess oil.

Nutrition: Calories: 320 Fat: 20g Carbs: 12g Protein: 24g

NOTES:

_____
_____
_____

29. Kaczka Pieczona: Roast Duck

Prep Time; 20 minutes

Cook time; 2 hours

Serves: 4

Ingredients:

- One whole duck (about 4 pounds)
- Salt and pepper to taste
- One orange, quartered
- One onion, quartered
- Four cloves of garlic, minced
- Two sprigs of fresh rosemary
- Two sprigs of fresh thyme

Directions:

1. Turn the temperature on the oven to 350 degrees Fahrenheit (175 degrees Celsius).

2. Duck should have any excess fat removed from it, and then it should be dried with paper towels. The duck should be well seasoned with salt and pepper.

3. Place the orange, onion, garlic, rosemary, and thyme inside the duck cavity.

4. Wrap the duck's legs in kitchen twine, and tuck its wings into its body so that they are flush with it.

5. Arrange the duck so that the breast side is facing up on a rack inside a roasting pan.

6. The duck should be roasted in the oven that has been preheated for two hours, or until a meat thermometer inserted into the thickest portion of the thigh registers an internal temperature of 165 degrees Fahrenheit (74 degrees Celsius).

7. Take the duck out of the oven and let it sit for ten minutes before attempting to carve it.

Nutrition (per serving): Calories: 275 Fat: 16g Carbs: 1g Protein: 30g

NOTES:

_____

_____

_____

30. Kotlety Mielone: Polish Meat Patties

Prep Time; 20 minutes

Cook time; 15 minutes

Serves: 4

Ingredients:

- 500g ground beef
- One medium onion, finely chopped
- One garlic clove, minced
- One-fourth cup bread crumbs
- One-fourth cup milk
- One egg
- One tsp. salt
- One-half tsp. black pepper
- One-half tsp. paprika
- One-fourth tsp. dried marjoram
- Vegetable oil, for frying

Directions:

1. Mix together the ground beef, chopped onion, minced garlic, bread crumbs, milk, egg, salt, black pepper, paprika, and dried marjoram in a large bowl. Season with salt and pepper to taste. Perform a full amalgamation of the constituent parts by thoroughly combining them all.

2. Form the mixture into patties that are roughly oval in form and approximately half an inch thick.

3. In a large skillet, bring the vegetable oil to a temperature of medium heat. After adding the beef patties, grill them for approximately 5-7 minutes on each side, or until they are well browned and cooked through.

4. Place the cooked patties on a dish that has been coated with paper towels so that they can soak up any remaining oil.

5. Serve the Kotlety Mielone hot with your favorite side dishes.

Nutrition (per serving): Calories: 300 Fat: 20g Carbs: 5g Protein: 25g

NOTES:

_____
_____
_____

Chapter 18. Traditional Polish Favorites:

31. Kartoflanka: Potato Soup

- Prep Time; 15 minutes
- Cook time; 30 minutes
- Serves: 4
- Ingredients:
- Four medium-sized potatoes, peeled and diced
- One large onion, finely chopped
- 2 cloves of garlic, minced
- 3 cups vegetable or chicken broth
- One cup milk or heavy cream
- 2 tbsp. butter
- One tsp. dried thyme
- Salt & pepper, as required
- Chopped fresh parsley, for garnish

Directions:

1. Butter will need to be melted in a big pot over medium heat. Add the garlic that has been minced and the chopped onion. Sauté the onion until it turns translucent and the garlic until it develops a fragrant flavor.

2. Put the diced potatoes in the pot and give everything a good stir. Cook for about 5 minutes, or until the potatoes have reached the desired degree of tenderness.

3. After you've done that, pour in the chicken or vegetable broth, and bring to a boil. Turn the heat down to a low setting and let it simmer for around twenty minutes, or until the potatoes are cooked through.

4. Using a potato masher or immersion blender, partially blend the soup to create a creamy yet chunky texture. If desired, you can also remove a portion of the soup and blend it separately before returning it to the pot.

5. After stirring in the milk or heavy cream, season the dish with salt, pepper, and dried thyme. Allow it to continue to cook for a few more minutes on low heat to ensure that the soup is completely heated.

6. Potato Soup, also known as Kartoflanka, should be served steaming hot and topped with finely chopped fresh parsley.

Nutrition (per serving): Calories: 250 Fat: 8g Carbs: 40g Protein: 6g

NOTES:

_____
_____
_____

32. Szarlotka: Polish Apple Pie

Prep Time; 30 minutes

Cook time; 45 minutes

Serves: 8

Ingredients:

- Two one-half cups all-purpose flour
- One cup unsalted butter, chilled and diced
- One-half cup granulated sugar
- One-fourth teaspoon salt
- Two large eggs
- 1 kg (about 8) apples, peeled, cored, and thinly sliced
- One-half cup granulated sugar
- One teaspoon ground cinnamon
- Juice of One-half lemon
- One-half cup breadcrumbs
- Powdered sugar for dusting

Directions:

1. Put the oven on to a temperature of 180 degrees Celsius (350 degrees Fahrenheit).

2. In a large mixing bowl, combine flour, diced butter, granulated sugar, and salt. Using your hands or a pastry cutter, mix the ingredients until crumbly.

3. After adding the egg, continue to knead the dough until it comes together. The dough should be cut in half, with one half being somewhat larger than the other.

4. The bigger piece of the dough should be rolled out and used to line the bottom and edges of a pie dish measuring 9 inches. Remove any surplus of dough.

5. Sliced apples, granulated sugar, ground cinnamon, and lemon juice should all be mixed together in a separate basin. To ensure that the apples are evenly coated, mix thoroughly.

6. Spread breadcrumbs over the bottom of the pie crust to prevent it from getting soggy.

7. Fill the pie crust with the apple mixture, spreading it evenly.

8. Roll out the remaining dough and cut it into strips. Arrange the strips over the apple filling, forming a lattice pattern.

9. In a bowl, beat what is left of the egg, and then brush it all over the lattice crust.

10. Bake in an oven that has been warmed for approximately forty-five minutes, or until the topping is golden brown and the apples are soft.

11. After it has finished baking, take it from the oven and wait until it has completely cooled before serving.

12. After it has been served, the pie should be dusted with powdered sugar.

Nutrition: Calories: 356 per serving (approximate values) Fat: 16g Carbs: 50g Protein: 4g

NOTES:
_____
_____
_____

33. Flaki: Tripe Soup

Prep Time; 30 minutes

Cook time; 2 hours

Serves: 4

Ingredients:

- 500g beef tripe, cleaned and cut into small pieces
- One onion, chopped
- Two carrots, diced
- Two celery stalks, diced
- Two cloves of garlic, minced
- Two bay leaves
- One tsp. dried marjoram
- One tsp. paprika
- One tbsp. tomato paste
- One liter beef broth
- Salt & pepper, as required
- Chopped fresh parsley for garnish

Directions:

1. Bring a big saucepan of water to a boil and set it aside. After adding the beef tripe, let the mixture to boil for five minutes. After draining the tripe, wash it well in ice water.

2. In the same saucepan, bring some oil up to temperature over a medium flame. Include the garlic, onion, carrots, and celery in the dish as well. Sauté the vegetables for a few minutes, or until they begin to get softer.

3. Return the beef tripe to the saucepan, then stir in the bay leaves, marjoram, paprika, and tomato paste. Season with salt and pepper to taste. Coat the tripe and veggies by thoroughly combining them in the mixture.

4. After pouring in the beef broth, reduce the heat to maintain a simmer. Turn the heat down to low and continue cooking the tripe for two hours, or until it reaches the desired tenderness.

5. Salt and pepper can be added to taste as a seasoning. Take the bay leaves out of the dish before serving.

6. Prepare the Flaki: Tripe Soup and serve it steaming hot, garnished with freshly chopped parsley.

Nutrition: (per serving) Calories: 250 Fat: 8g Carbs: 12g Protein: 30g

34. Placki Ziemniaczane: Potato Pancakes

Prep Time; 15 minutes

Cook time; 10 minutes

Serves: 4

Ingredients:

- Four large potatoes
- One small onion
- Two eggs
- Two tbsp. all-purpose flour
- One tsp. salt
- One-fourth tsp. pepper
- Vegetable oil for frying

Directions:

1. You can use a box grater or a food processor to shred the potatoes and the onion. To remove any excess moisture from the grated potatoes and onion, use a kitchen towel or cheesecloth and squeeze the ingredients.

2. Mix the grated potatoes, onion, eggs, flour, salt, and pepper in a large bowl. Add the ingredients in order. Perform a thorough mixing until everything is uniformly distributed.

3. In a frying pan, bring some vegetable oil up to temperature over medium heat.

4. Take a portion of the potato mixture and place it in the hot oil, then use a spatula to slightly flatten it. Repeat this process. Continue with the remaining scoops, making sure to leave some room in between each pancake.

5. Cook the potato pancakes for approximately three to four minutes on each side, or until they are crisp and golden brown. Using a spatula, carefully turn the pancakes over.

6. Take the potato pancakes out of the pan once they are done cooking and lay them on a dish lined with paper towels to soak up any excess oil.

7. Serve the Placki Ziemniaczane hot with sour cream or applesauce.

Nutrition: Calories 200 Fat 8g Carbs 28g Protein 5g

NOTES:

_____
_____
_____

35. Pyzy: Potato Dumplings

Prep Time; 30 minutes

Cook time; 20 minutes

Serves: 4

Ingredients:

- Two large potatoes, peeled and boiled
- One cup all-purpose flour
- One egg
- Salt and pepper to taste
- Optional: One tbsp. grated onion
- Optional: One tbsp. chopped fresh parsley

Directions:

1. In a large mixing bowl, mash the boiled potatoes until smooth.

2. Add the flour, egg, salt, pepper, grated onion, and chopped parsley (if using) to the mashed potatoes. Mix well until all the ingredients are combined.

3. Take small portions of the dough and roll them into small balls, about 1-2 inches in diameter.

4. Bring a large pot of salted water to a boil. Drop the potato dumplings into the boiling water and cook for about 10-15 minutes, or until they float to the surface.

5. Remove the cooked dumplings from the water using a slotted spoon and drain any excess water.

6. Serve the pyzy hot with your favorite sauce or topping.

Nutrition (per serving): Calories: 250 Fat: 2g Carbs: 52g Protein: 6g

NOTES:

36. Krupnik: Polish Barley Soup

Prep Time; 15 minutes

Cook time; One hour 30 minutes

Serves: 6

Ingredients:

- One cup pearl barley
- Eight cups vegetable broth
- Three medium potatoes, peeled and diced
- Two large carrots, peeled and diced
- One large onion, chopped
- Two cloves garlic, minced
- Two tbsp. olive oil
- One bay leaf
- One tsp. dried thyme
- One tsp. dried marjoram
- Salt & pepper, as required
- Chopped fresh parsley for garnish

Directions:

1. Rinse the pearl barley under cold water and drain.

2. The olive oil should be heated in a large saucepan over medium heat. Add the garlic that has been minced and the chopped onion. Sauté the onion until it turns a transparent color.

3. After adding the carrots in diced form, continue cooking for another 5 minutes while swirling the pan occasionally.

4. In a large pot, combine the pearl barley, chopped potatoes, bay leaf, dried thyme, dried marjoram, salt, and pepper. Mix to ensure a complete blending.

5. The vegetable broth should then be poured in and the pot should be brought to a boil. Cover the saucepan, reduce the heat to low, and let it simmer for about an hour, or until the barley is soft.

6. Taste and adjust the seasoning if needed.

7. Remove the bay leaf before serving.

8. Place a serving of the Krupnik soup in each bowl, then top with some finely chopped fresh parsley.

Nutrition (per serving): Calories: 250 Fat: 5g Carbs: 45g Protein: 7g

37. Kielbasa z Kapustą: Sausage with Sauerkraut

Prep Time; 15 minutes

Cook time; One hour

Serves: 4

Ingredients:

- One pound kielbasa sausage
- One onion, chopped
- One clove garlic, minced
- One pound sauerkraut, drained
- One-half cup chicken broth
- One tsp. caraway seeds
- One tsp. paprika
- Salt & pepper, as required

Directions:

1. Start by heating some oil in a big skillet over a medium flame. After adding the kielbasa sausage, continue to cook it until it has a browned appearance on all sides. Take the food out of the skillet and set it aside.

2. Place the chopped onion and garlic that has been minced into the same skillet. Cook the onion until it turns a transparent color.

3. In a skillet over medium heat, combine the sauerkraut, chicken broth, caraway seeds, paprika, and seasonings of your choice. Mix to ensure a complete blending.

4. Bring the kielbasa back into the pan it was cooked in. Cover and cook over low heat for one hour, stirring occasionally, or until the sauerkraut is soft and the flavors have melded together.

5. Serve the Kielbasa z Kapustą hot, with mashed potatoes or crusty bread on the side.

Nutrition (per serving): Calories: 420 Fat: 32g Carbs: 8g Protein: 15g

NOTES:

_____
_____
_____

38. Kaczka w Sosie Miodowo-Musztardowym: Duck in Honey Mustard Sauce

Prep Time; 20 minutes

Cook time; 2 hours

Serves: 4

Ingredients:

- One whole duck (about 4-5 pounds)
- One-fourth cup honey
- One-fourth cup Dijon mustard
- Two cloves garlic, minced
- One tbsp. soy sauce
- Salt & pepper, as required

Directions:

1. Turn the temperature on the oven to 350 degrees Fahrenheit (175 degrees Celsius).

2. Honey, mustard made with Dijon, minced garlic, soy sauce, salt, and pepper should be combined in a small basin and stirred together.

3. Put the duck on a chopping board, and use some paper towels to thoroughly dry it off. Salt and pepper should be used to season the duck..

4. Some oil should be heated over medium heat in a big roasting pan or skillet that can go in the oven. After placing the duck in the pan with the breast side down, sear it for about four to five minutes, or until it has a golden brown color. After searing one side of the duck for four to five minutes, turn it over and continue cooking.

5. Take the duck out of the skillet and dispose of any excess fat that has accumulated. Put the duck back in the pan, this time with the breast side facing up. The honey mustard sauce should be brushed over the duck, and careful attention should be paid to ensure that it is coated uniformly.

6. Roast the duck for approximately two hours, or until the internal temperature reaches 165 degrees Fahrenheit (75 degrees Celsius), after transferring the skillet to an oven that has been prepared. At thirty minute intervals, baste the duck with the fluids that have accumulated in the pan.

7. After it has finished cooking, take the duck out of the oven and allow it to rest for ten to fifteen minutes before carving.

8. Serve the duck with the remaining honey mustard sauce on the side.

9. Enjoy your Kaczka w Sosie Miodowo-Musztardowym!

Nutrition (per serving): Calories: 420 Fat: 28g Carbs: 8g Protein: 32g

39. Barszcz Wigilijny: Christmas Eve Beet Soup

Prep Time; 30 minutes

Cook time; 2 hours

Serves: 6

Ingredients:

- Four medium beets, peeled and grated
- One onion, finely chopped
- Four cloves garlic, minced
- Four cups vegetable broth
- One tbsp. apple cider vinegar
- One tbsp. honey or sugar (optional)
- Salt & pepper, as required
- Sour cream or yogurt for garnish (optional)
- Fresh dill for garnish (optional)

Directions:

1. The onion and garlic should be cooked over a medium heat in a large pot until the onion becomes transparent.

2. Grate the beets and add them to the pot. Cook for five minutes while stirring the mixture occasionally.

3. The vegetable broth should then be poured in and the pot should be brought to a boil. Bring the temperature down to a gentle simmer and cook for an hour.

4. Mix in the honey or sugar if you're using it, as well as the apple cider vinegar. Salt and pepper can be added to taste as a seasoning.

5. Keep the pot on low heat and simmer for another half an hour to enable the flavors to come together.

6. Take the soup off the stove and let it cool down a little bit.

7. Use either a regular blender or an immersion blender to purée the soup until it is completely smooth. You also have the option of leaving it relatively chunky if that is what you like.

8. Place the soup back in the saucepan and, if required, reheat it.

9. Serve hot, and if you choose, top each portion with a dollop of sour cream or yogurt and some fresh dill.

Nutrition (per serving): Calories: 150 Fat: 1g Carbs: 35g Protein: 4g

42. Karp Pieczony: Baked Carp

Prep Time; 30 minutes

Cook time; One hour

Serves: 4

Ingredients:

- One whole carp, cleaned and gutted
- Two tablespoons olive oil
- Salt and pepper to taste
- One lemon, sliced
- Two cloves garlic, minced
- One tbsp. chopped fresh parsley
- One tbsp. chopped fresh dill
- One tbsp. chopped fresh thyme
- One tbsp. butter, melted

Directions:

1. Set the temperature in the oven to 375 degrees Fahrenheit (190 degrees Celsius).

2. Carp should be washed under cold water and then dried off with paper towels.

3. Carp should be rubbed with olive oil before being placed on a big baking sheet and cooking. Both the inside and the outside of the fish should be seasoned with salt and pepper.

4. Stuff the cavity of the carp with lemon slices, minced garlic, parsley, dill, and thyme.

5. Brush the melted butter over the carp.

6. Carp should be baked in an oven that has been prepared for 45 to 60 minutes, or until it is completely cooked through and flakes readily when tested with a fork.

7. Take the carp out of the oven and let it sit for a few minutes to let the flavors settle before serving.

8. Serve the baked carp with lemon wedges and garnish with fresh herbs.

Nutrition: Calories: 250 per serving Fat: 10g Carbs: 2g Protein: 36g

NOTES:

_____
_____
_____

43. Kaszanka: Polish Black Pudding

Prep Time; 20 minutes

Cook time; 40 minutes

Serves: 4

Ingredients:

- One lb pork liver
- One lb pork blood
- One lb pork fatback or bacon
- One large onion, finely chopped
- Two cloves garlic, minced
- One tsp. salt
- One-half tsp. black pepper
- One-half tsp. marjoram
- One-fourth tsp. ground allspice
- One-fourth tsp. ground cloves
- One cup cooked rice (optional, for texture)

Directions:

1. Bring a big saucepan of water to a boil and set it aside. After adding the pork liver, let it cook for around twenty minutes, or until it is soft. Take it out of the saucepan and let it to cool.

2. Once cooled, finely chop the pork liver and set aside.

3. Cook the pork fatback or the bacon in a separate pan until it is nice and crispy. Take it out of the pan, and then let it cool down. After it has gotten cold, cut it up into little pieces.

4. In the same pan, sauté the onion and garlic until golden brown.

5. In a large bowl, combine the chopped pork liver, cooked chopped fatback or bacon, sautéed onion, garlic, salt, black pepper, marjoram, allspice, and cloves. Mix well to combine.

6. Gradually add the pork blood while stirring continuously.

7. If desired, stir in the cooked rice for texture.

8. Put some oil or lard in a baking dish and then pour the ingredients into it. Bake at 350 degrees for 30 minutes.

9. Cook the kaszanka in an oven that has been prepared to 350 degrees Fahrenheit (175 degrees Celsius) for approximately 40 minutes, or until it is firm and browned.

10. Take it out of the oven and wait until it has cooled down a little bit before slicing.

Nutrition (per serving): Calories: 350 Fat: 25g Carbs: 7g Protein: 23g

46. Sledzie po Kaszubsku: Herring Kaszubski Style

Prep Time; 20 minutes

Cook time; 30 minutes

Serves: 4

Ingredients:

- 500g herring fillets
- One onion, thinly sliced
- Two tbsp. vegetable oil
- Two tbsp. cider vinegar
- One tbsp. sugar
- One tsp. black peppercorns
- Four bay leaves
- Four allspice berries
- Four cloves
- One red apple, peeled and grated
- One carrot, peeled and grated
- One pickled cucumber, finely chopped
- Fresh dill, for garnish

Directions:

1. Mix the chopped onion, cider vinegar, sugar, black peppercorns, allspice berries, and cloves together in a bowl of medium size. Combine thoroughly and then set aside.

2. After being washed in ice-cold water, the herring fillets should be dried off using a paper towel. They should be cut into large pieces and then placed in a dish made of glass.

3. The herring fillets should be completely covered with the onion mixture after it has been poured on top of them. Wrap the dish in plastic wrap, place it in the refrigerator, and let it sit there for at least four hours or overnight.

4. After the allotted time has passed, the herring should be removed from the dish, and the marinade should be thrown away.

5. Warm the vegetable oil in a large skillet by heating it over a medium flame. After about three to four minutes on each side, add the herring fillets to the pan and cook them until they are brown and crispy. Take them out of the pan, and then set them aside to cool.

6. Once cooled, arrange the herring fillets on a serving platter. Top them with grated apple, grated carrot, and chopped pickled cucumber.

7. Garnish with fresh dill and serve chilled.

Nutrition (per serving): Calories: 280 Fat: 15g Carbs: 11g Protein: 25g

47. Sledzie w Oleju: Herring in Oil

Prep Time; 30 minutes

Cook time; 10 minutes

Serves: 4

Ingredients:

- 500g fresh herring fillets
- One cup white vinegar
- One cup water
- One onion, thinly sliced
- 2 bay leaves
- 6 whole black peppercorns
- 4 cloves
- One tsp. sugar
- One tsp. salt
- One cup vegetable oil

Directions:

1. After being washed in ice-cold water, the herring fillets should be dried thoroughly using paper towels.

2. Put the vinegar, water, onion, bay leaves, peppercorns, cloves, sugar, and salt into a saucepan and stir to mix everything. Bring the concoction up to a rolling boil.

3. Cook the herring fillets for five minutes after adding them to the fluid that is already boiling. Take it off the heat and let it cool down.

4. Once cooled, transfer the herring fillets along with the onion slices to a glass jar or airtight container.

5. Pour the vegetable oil over the herring fillets, making sure they are completely submerged.

6. Before serving, ensure the container is airtight and that it has been chilled for at least 24 hours.

Nutrition: Calories: 280 calories Fat: 25g Carbs: 2g Protein: 12g

NOTES:

_____
_____
_____

48. Kaczka w Sosie Jablkowym: Duck in Apple Sauce

Prep Time; 20 minutes

Cook time; 2 hours

Serves: 4

Ingredients:

- One whole duck (about 4-5 pounds)
- Two apples, peeled, cored, and sliced
- One onion, finely chopped
- Two cloves of garlic, minced
- One cup apple juice or cider
- One-fourth cup apple cider vinegar
- Two tbsp. honey
- Two tbsp. Dijon mustard
- One tbsp. fresh thyme leaves
- Salt & pepper, as required

Directions:

1. Turn the temperature on the oven to 350 degrees Fahrenheit (175 degrees Celsius).

2. Duck is seasoned with salt and pepper after being dried with paper towels and then patted dry.

3. The breast side of the duck should face down when it is placed in a large ovenproof skillet. Cook for about ten minutes over medium-high heat, turning occasionally, until the skin is browned and crispy. Cook for an extra 5 minutes after you have flipped the duck.

4. Take the duck out of the skillet and put it to the side for later. Remove the extra fat from the skillet and save aside approximately 2 tablespoons of the fat.

5. After adding the garlic and onions to the pan, allow them to cook for about 5 minutes, or until the onions are translucent and the garlic is gently browned.

6. Mix in the apple slices, apple juice, apple cider vinegar, honey, Dijon mustard, thyme leaves, and a pinch each of salt and pepper before serving. Raise the temperature to a simmer with the mixture.

7. Place the duck back into the pan with the breast side facing up. Put something heavy on top of the skillet, such a lid or some aluminum foil, and place it in the oven after it has been preheated.

8. The duck should be baked for approximately one hour and thirty minutes, or until the thickest section of the thigh reaches an internal temperature of 165 degrees Fahrenheit (74 degrees Celsius).

9. Take the cast iron pan out of the oven and place the duck on a chopping board. After letting it rest for ten minutes, you can begin cutting it.

10. While everything is going on, pour the sauce that was in the skillet into a separate saucepan. Remove any extra fat, then place the sauce in a saucepan and simmer it over medium heat for about five minutes, or until it begins to thicken slightly.

11. Carve the duck into serving pieces and serve with the apple sauce on the side. Drizzle the duck with the reduced sauce.

12. Enjoy your Kaczka w Sosie Jablkowym: Duck in Apple Sauce!

Nutrition: (per serving) Calories: 450 Fat: 20g Carbs: 18gProtein: 45g

NOTES:

_____
_____
_____

49. Miruna: Herring Salad

Prep Time; 15 minutes

Cook time; 0 minutes

Serves: 4

Ingredients:

- Eight ounces herring fillets, skinless and boneless
- One small red onion, thinly sliced
- One cucumber, thinly sliced
- Two small apples, cored and diced
- Two tbsp. fresh dill, chopped
- Two tbsp. lemon juice
- Two tbsp. olive oil
- Salt & pepper, as required

Directions:

1. Mix the sliced red onion, cucumber, diced apples, and chopped dill together in a medium bowl.

2. Herring fillets should be cut into pieces that are easily digestible, and then they should be added to the bowl.

3. In a second, more intimate bowl, combine the lemon juice, olive oil, salt, and pepper in a whisking motion.

4. After pouring the dressing over the salad ingredients, gently toss everything together.

5. Before serving, let the salad to sit in the refrigerator for at least half an hour so that the flavors can combine.

6. Serve the Miruna Herring Salad chilled as a delicious and refreshing appetizer or side dish.

Nutrition (per serving): Calories: 210 Fat: 11g Carbs: 11g Protein: 17g

NOTES:

_____
_____
_____

50. Krewetki Curry: Shrimp Curry

Prep Time; 15 minutes

Cook time; 20 minutes

Serves: 4

Ingredients:

- 500g shrimp, peeled and deveined
- One onion, finely chopped
- Two garlic cloves, minced
- One red bell pepper, diced
- Two tbsp. curry powder
- One tsp. turmeric powder
- One can (400ml) coconut milk
- Two tbsp. vegetable oil
- Salt & pepper, as required
- Chopped cilantro for garnish
- Cooked rice or naan bread for serving

Directions:

1. In a large skillet, bring the vegetable oil to a temperature of medium heat. Add the garlic that has been minced and the chopped onion. Sauté the onion until it reaches a transparent state.

2. Dice the bell pepper and add it to the skillet. Continue to cook for another two to three minutes, or until the pepper begins to soften.

3. Sprinkle the curry powder and turmeric powder over the vegetables. Stir well to coat.

4. Put the shrimp in the pan and cook them for about three to four minutes, or until they become pink and are opaque all the way through.

5. Pour the coconut milk into the bowl, then season it with the pepper and salt. To mix everything together, stir.

6. Turn the stove down to a low setting and let the curry simmer for ten minutes, which will allow the flavors to meld together.

7. Try it out, then make any necessary adjustments to the seasoning.

8. Serve the shrimp curry over cooked rice or with naan bread. Garnish with chopped cilantro.

Nutrition (per serving): Calories: 320 Fat: 22g Carbs: 10g Protein: 24g

53. Kopytka: Polish Potato Dumplings

Prep Time; 40 minutes

Cook time; 15 minutes

Serves: 4

Ingredients:

- 500g potatoes, peeled and boiled
- 200g all-purpose flour
- One egg
- One tsp. salt
- Optional toppings: butter, breadcrumbs, sour cream

Directions:

1. Mash the boiled potatoes until smooth.

2. Mix the mashed potatoes, flour, egg, and salt together in a bowl before adding them to the bowl. Continue to blend in a mixer until a dough ball is formed.

3. Cut the dough into small pieces and roll it into ropes with a thickness of about one centimeter.

4. Reduce the ropes to smaller pieces, each measuring two centimeters in length.

5. Start the cooking process by bringing a large pot of salted water to a boil. After around three to five minutes, when the dumplings have reached the surface of the liquid, add them.

6. Using a slotted spoon, lift the dumplings out of the water, and arrange them on a platter that is intended for serving.

7. If you want the dumplings to have a golden crust, you can add a little butter to a skillet, melt it, and then lightly sauté the cooked dumplings. You also have the option of topping them with breadcrumbs before lightly toasting them in the oven.

8. Serve the kopytka hot with your choice of toppings, such as butter, breadcrumbs, or sour cream.

Nutrition (per serving): Calories: 300 Fat: 5g Carbs: 55g Protein: 8g

NOTES:

_____
_____
_____

54. Placki z Jabłkami: Apple Pancakes

Prep Time; 15 minutes

Cook time; 15 minutes

Serves: 4

Ingredients:

- 2 cups all-purpose flour
- One-fourth cup granulated sugar
- Two tsp. baking powder
- One-half tsp. salt
- One-half tsp. ground cinnamon
- One cup milk
- Two large eggs
- Two medium-sized apples, peeled, cored, and grated
- Two tbsp. unsalted butter, melted
- Vegetable oil for frying

Directions:

1. Flour, sugar, baking powder, salt, and ground cinnamon should be mixed together in a large basin using a whisking motion.

2. The milk, eggs, grated apples, and melted butter should each be combined in their own bowl and whisked together.

3. After pouring the liquid components into the bowl containing the dry ingredients, give it a little swirl until everything is just incorporated. Take care not to overmix.

4. Heat a frying pan over medium heat and add enough vegetable oil to coat the bottom.

5. Using a 1/4 cup measuring cup, scoop the batter onto the hot pan. Flatten the batter gently with the back of a spoon.

6. Cook for about two to three minutes on each side, or until the edges of the pancakes are golden brown and the pancakes have set.

7. Transfer the cooked pancakes to a paper towel-lined plate to remove excess oil.

8. Repeat steps 5-7 with the remaining batter, adding more oil to the pan as needed.

9. Serve the Placki z Jabłkami warm with your choice of toppings such as powdered sugar, honey, or maple syrup.

Nutrition (per serving): Calories: 250 Fat: 8g Carbs: 38g Protein: 6g

55. Cwikla: Polish Beetroot Horseradish Relish

Prep Time; 15 minutes

Cook time; 45 minutes

Serves: 4

Ingredients:

- 500g beetroots, peeled and grated
- One small onion, finely chopped
- Two cloves of garlic, minced
- 3 tablespoons horseradish, grated
- Two tbsp. white wine vinegar
- One tbsp. sugar
- One tsp. salt
- One-fourth tsp. black pepper

Directions:

1. Mix the grated beetroots, chopped onion, minced garlic, grated horseradish, white wine vinegar, sugar, salt, and black pepper together in a large bowl. Make sure everything is well-combined by giving it a thorough mix.

2. Place the contents of the bowl into a large saucepan, then bring the water to a boil over medium heat. Turn the heat down to low and continue to simmer the beetroots for around 45 minutes, stirring the mixture regularly, until the beetroots are soft and the flavors have melded together.

3. Take the Cwikla off the heat, and let it to come down to room temperature. Transfer to a jar or other airtight container, and place in the refrigerator for at least two hours before serving in order to give the flavors time to meld.

4. Serve the Cwikla as a condiment or side dish with grilled meats, sausages, or as a topping for sandwiches.

Nutrition per serving (approximately): Calories: 96 Fat: 0.3g Carbs: 23.4g Protein: 2.4g

NOTES:

56. Kwasnica: Polish Sauerkraut

Prep Time; 15 minutes

Cook time; 2 hours

Serves: 6

Ingredients:

- One head of cabbage, shredded
- One large onion, chopped
- Three cloves of garlic, minced
- One pound of smoked sausage, sliced
- Four cups of chicken broth
- Two tbsp. of vegetable oil
- One tsp. of caraway seeds
- Salt & pepper, as required

Directions:

1. In a big pot, bring the vegetable oil to a temperature of medium heat. After adding the onions and garlic, continue to sauté them for around 5 minutes, or until they become translucent.

2. After adding the sliced sausage to the pot, wait around 5 minutes for it to become browned before moving it on to the next step.

3. In a pot, combine the shredded cabbage, caraway seeds, salt, and pepper by giving everything a thorough toss before serving. Continue to cook for another 5 minutes, stirring a few times during that time.

4. Pour the chicken broth into the pot, then bring everything else to a boil. Put a lid on the pot, reduce the heat to low, and let it simmer for about two hours, or until the cabbage is fork-tender.

5. Serve hot and enjoy!

Nutrition: Calories: 320 Fat: 20g Carbs: 15g Protein: 18g

NOTES:

_____
_____
_____

57. Racuchy: Polish Yeast Pancakes

Prep Time; 15 minutes

Cook time; 20 minutes

Serves: 4

Ingredients:

- 250g all-purpose flour
- One-half tsp. salt
- 1 tbsp. granulated sugar
- One-half tsp. active dry yeast
- 250ml lukewarm milk
- Two large eggs
- Two tbsp. melted butter
- Vegetable oil, for frying
- Powdered sugar, for dusting

Directions:

1. Put the flour, salt, sugar, and yeast into a bowl and mix them together.

2. Gradually add lukewarm milk while stirring until a smooth batter forms.

3. Allow the batter to rise for an additional hour in a warm location while the bowl is covered with a dish towel.

4. After the batter has risen, whisk in the eggs and melted butter until well combined.

5. In a frying pan, bring the oil from a vegetable source up to a medium temperature.

6. Spoon about 2 tablespoons of the batter into the pan for each pancake.

7. Cook the pancakes for 2-3 minutes on each side until golden brown.

8. Transfer the cooked pancakes to a paper towel-lined plate to remove excess oil.

9. Dust the pancakes with powdered sugar before serving.

Nutrition (per serving): Calories: 280 Fat: 9g Carbs: 39g Protein: 9g

NOTES:

_____
_____
_____

58. Kiszona Kapusta: Fermented Sauerkraut

Prep Time; 30 minutes

Cook time; 2 hours

Serves: 6

Ingredients:

- Two kg cabbage, finely shredded
- 2-3 tbsp. sea salt
- One tsp. caraway seeds
- One tsp. juniper berries (optional)
- 5-6 cloves garlic, minced
- One tbsp. grated ginger (optional)

Directions:

1. Shaved cabbage and a generous amount of salt should be combined in a big bowl. Use your hands to knead the cabbage for around five to ten minutes, or until it begins to lose its liquid.

2. Add the caraway seeds, juniper berries (if using), minced garlic, and grated ginger (if using) to the cabbage. Be sure to blend everything thoroughly.

3. Transfer the cabbage mixture to a fermentation vessel, such as a glass jar or fermenting crock. Press the cabbage down firmly to release any trapped air bubbles.

4. If there is not enough liquid to cover the cabbage, prepare a brine by dissolving 1-2 tablespoons of sea salt in 1 liter of filtered water. Pour enough brine over the cabbage to cover it completely.

5. Place a weight on top of the cabbage to keep it submerged in the brine. This can be a small plate or a jar filled with water.

6. Cover the fermentation vessel with a lid or cloth to protect it from dust and insects.

7. At a minimum of 14 days, the sauerkraut needs to be allowed to ferment at room temperature. Check it regularly to make sure the cabbage remains submerged and there is no mold forming on the surface. Skim off any scum that may appear.

8. After 2 weeks, taste the sauerkraut. If it has reached the desired level of tanginess, it is ready to be transferred to the refrigerator for long-term storage. If you prefer a stronger flavor, you can let it ferment for a few more days.

9. Store the fermented sauerkraut in the refrigerator, where it will continue to slowly ferment and develop more flavor over time.

Nutrition (per serving): Calories: 35 Fat: 0g Carbs: 8g Protein: 1g

59. Zapiekanka: Polish Baguette Pizza

Prep Time; 15 minutes

Cook time; 20 minutes

Serves: 4

Ingredients:

- One French baguette
- 200g mushrooms, sliced
- One onion, thinly sliced
- 200g grated cheese (cheddar or mozzarella)
- Four tbsp ketchup
- Two tbsp. mayonnaise
- Salt & pepper, as required

Directions:

1. Put the oven on to a temperature of 200 degrees Celsius (400 degrees Fahrenheit).

2. The baguette should be cut in half lengthwise, and both halves should be placed on a baking sheet.

3. Cook the mushrooms and onions over medium heat in a skillet with a bit of oil until they begin to break down and release their liquid. Add little salt and pepper before serving.

4. Spread the ketchup evenly on the baguette halves.

5. Top the baguette halves with the sautéed mushrooms and onions.

6. Sprinkle the grated cheese over the toppings.

7. Bake in an oven that has been warmed for approximately fifteen to twenty minutes, or until the cheese completely melts and turns golden brown.

8. Take it out of the oven and let it cool for a little while.

9. Drizzle mayonnaise over the Zapiekanka.

10. Cut into individual portions and serve hot.

Nutrition (per serving): Calories: 350 Fat: 12g Carbs: 45g Protein: 15g

NOTES:

_____
_____
_____

60. Surówka z Kapusty: Coleslaw

Prep Time; 15 minutes

Cook time; Not required

Serves: 4

Ingredients:

- One small head of cabbage, shredded
- Two carrots, grated
- One small onion, finely chopped
- One-half cup mayonnaise
- Two tbsp. white vinegar
- One tbsp. sugar
- Salt & pepper, as required

Directions:

1. Shredded cabbage, grated carrots, and chopped onion should all be mixed together in a big basin.

2. Mayonnaise, white vinegar, sugar, salt, and pepper should all be mixed together in a separate, smaller bowl until they are completely incorporated.

3. After pouring the dressing over the cabbage mixture, toss everything together until it is well covered.

4. Before serving, cover the bowl and place it in the refrigerator for at least an hour. This will allow the flavors to combine and become more pronounced.

5. Serve cold, and have fun with it!

Nutrition (per serving): Calories: 180 Fat: 11g Carbs: 19g Protein: 2g

NOTES:

_____
_____
_____

Conclusion

Thank you for making it to the end. A Polish cookbook offers a delightful culinary journey through the rich and diverse flavors of Polish cuisine. To ensure success in creating authentic and delicious Polish dishes, consider the following tips:

1. Embrace the key ingredients: Polish cuisine relies heavily on staple ingredients like potatoes, cabbage, onions, beets, mushrooms, and various meats. By using fresh, high-quality produce, you can elevate the flavors of your dishes.

2. Pay attention to seasonality: Polish cuisine is deeply rooted in seasonal ingredients. Try to incorporate seasonal produce and adjust recipes accordingly to make the most of the natural flavors each season has to offer.

3. Master the art of pickling: Pickled vegetables, such as sauerkraut and cucumber pickles, are essential in Polish cooking. Experiment with different pickling techniques to achieve the perfect balance of tanginess and crunchiness.

4. Don't forget the herbs and spices: Polish recipes often use a combination of herbs and spices, such as dill, marjoram, caraway seeds, and paprika. These aromatic ingredients add depth and complexity to many Polish dishes.

5. Explore traditional Polish cooking methods: Polish cuisine includes various cooking techniques, such as braising, baking, and sautéing. Familiarize yourself with these methods and apply them correctly to ensure the best results.

6. Respect the tradition, but be open to innovation: While Polish cooking holds strong ties to tradition, don't be afraid to put your own twist on classic recipes. Experiment with modern twists, ingredient substitutions, and presentation styles to create unique and contemporary Polish dishes.

7. Enjoy with traditional accompaniments: Polish cuisine often features accompaniments like sour cream, horseradish, mustard, and rye bread. These condiments enhance the flavors and bring authenticity to your Polish meals.

8. Appreciate the diversity of Polish desserts: Polish desserts range from delicate pastries like paczki and babka to heartier sweets like apple strudel and gingerbread. Explore the wide array of Polish desserts and indulge in the sweet side of Polish cuisine.

By following these tips, you will be well-equipped to create a tantalizing Polish culinary experience for yourself and your loved ones. So, grab your apron, gather your ingredients, and embark on a delicious journey through the flavors of Poland!

I hope you liked this book!